Mind Hacking:

Stoicism & Photographic Memory book. Discover Accelerated Learning Techniques to Unlock your Full Potential. Gain Self Confidence and Gain Unlimited Memory. Emotional Inteligence

Stoicism:

Stoic Way of Life, Stoicism Philosophy & Wisdom. Create Life Long Habits of Mental Toughness, Self Discipline. Master Self Confidence. Control Your Emotions. Anger Management and Jelousy.

Table of Contents

Introduction...6
Chapter 1: What is Stoicism?....................................8
Chapter 2: The History of Stoicism.........................18
Chapter 3: How to Become an Unbiased Thinker..................23
Chapter 4: The Importance of Fortitude and Self-Control...28
Chapter 5: Using Stoicism to Become Free From Jealousy, Greed, and Anger...30
Chapter 6: How to Overcome Destructive Emotions...37
Chapter 7: How to Use Stoicism to Take On the Negativity In Your Life..42
Chapter 8: How to Recognize Stoicism in Your Modern Life...45
Chapter 9: The Stoic Methods to Helping Improve Your Modern Life...52
Chapter 10: Why Should I Implement Stoicism in My Life?..60
Chapter 11: Is It Possible to Become Too Stoic?....................68
Chapter 12: How to use Stoicism for the Long Term and Planning Your Future as a Stoic.............................71
Conclusion..79

© Copyright 2019 by Luke Caldwell - All rights reserved.
This Book is provided with the sole purpose of providing relevant information on a specific topic for which every reasonable effort has been made to ensure that it is both accurate and reasonable. Nevertheless, by purchasing this Book you consent to the fact that the author, as well as the publisher, are in no way experts on the topics contained herein, regardless of any claims as such that may be made within. As such, any suggestions or recommendations that are made within are done so purely for entertainment value. It is recommended that you always consult a professional prior to undertaking any of the advice or techniques discussed within.
This is a legally binding declaration that is considered both valid and fair by both the Committee of Publishers Association and the American Bar Association and should be considered as legally binding within the United States.

The reproduction, transmission, and duplication of any of the content found herein, including any specific or extended information will be done as an illegal act regardless of the end form the information ultimately takes. This includes copied versions of the work both physical, digital and audio unless express consent of the Publisher is provided beforehand. Any additional rights reserved.

Furthermore, the information that can be found within the pages described forthwith shall be considered both accurate and truthful when it comes to the recounting of facts. As such, any use, correct or incorrect, of the provided information will render the Publisher free of responsibility as to the actions taken outside of their direct purview. Regardless, there are zero scenarios where the original author or the Publisher can be deemed liable in any fashion for any damages or hardships that may result from any of the information discussed herein.

Additionally, the information in the following pages is intended only for informational purposes and should thus be thought of as universal. As befitting its nature, it is presented without assurance regarding its prolonged validity or interim quality. Trademarks that are mentioned are done without written consent and can in no way be considered an endorsement from the trademark holder.

Introduction

Congratulations on downloading *Stoicism* and thank you for doing so.

The following chapters will discuss everything that you need to know in order to get started with Stoicism. Stoicism is a great philosophy to follow. It helps you to recognize more about your emotions and how they work, and ensures that you are able to maintain control, and choose when to express your emotions, and be the one in charge of your emotions. Most people choose to just let their emotions taking over, getting mad when things don't go their way. but this can lead to ruined relationships, missed opportunities, and so much more.

This guidebook is all about Stoicism and how you can implement this theology into your own life. We will take a look at some of the basics of Stoicism, the history that comes with Stoicism, and how you can use this ideology to help improve so much of your modern life. You can learn about how destructive emotions can get in the way of your happy life and how Stoicism can help you to learn more self-control, how to become an unbiased thinker, and how to use it to get rid of all the negativity that is already in your life.

There is a lot of miscommunication when it comes to working with Stoicism. Many people who have never taken a look through this school of thought think that Stoics have no emotions and are cold, but in reality, Stoics have the same emotions at others, they just choose to have full control over how they use those emotions, which leads to a much fuller and happier life. When you are ready to learn more about Stoicism and how you can use it to improve your life, make sure to read through this guidebook to learn how to get started.

There are plenty of books on this subject on the market, so thanks again for choosing this one! Every effort was made to ensure it is full of as much useful information as possible. Please enjoy!

Chapter 1: What is Stoicism?

Stoicism, or the stoic philosophy, may seem boring to a lot of people. Or perhaps you hear those words and think that it is a daunting task to even begin to understand what is going on with this school of thought. But in reality, the principles that come with Stoicism are pretty easy to work with and understand and implementing them into our modern lives can help us to grow, improve, gain more control over our emotions, and so much more.

Stoicism is a way of life. It teaches you how you can keep a rational and calm mind, no matter what is going on around you. Many times, we feel that our lives are in turmoil. Things just aren't going our way. We think that everyone is constantly mad at us. We think that people are against us. We lose our temper, never get things done, and often feel like a failure in the process.

But with Stoicism, we learn to think about things in a different way. We learn that we can have control, and it is easier than we could imagine. For example, how many times have you let your emotions get the best of you? You got angry about something, frustrated, sad, or even happy, and just couldn't get the emotion to stop. You yelled and screamed, got in a fight, started throwing things, and felt like everything was out of your control.

This kind of thinking is very dangerous. It makes us feel in discord to other things that are going on around us, and can make us feel bad, anxious, and stressed out. Even though we may feel like we are out of control in this situation, we actually have all the control in the world.

In this guidebook, we are going to spend a lot of time looking at Stoicism and all the different parts that come with it. But one of the underlying ideas that are there is that we have control. Sure, an emotion does come up and we can't stop our feelings. But we can take a look at that emotion and logically think of how we want to react to it.

When we are angry, we don't have to lash out at others. We can acknowledge that the emotion is there, determine whether it is valid or not, and then decide how we want to react. Once you realize that you have all the power in the world over your life, things don't seem as chaotic or crazy any longer. Yes, you will still have emotions, but you will learn how to have control over them, rather than them having all the control over you. Of course, this is just one of the ideas that come with Stoicism. Stoicism goes against some of the modern ideas that many of us hold dear. It realizes that there are a lot of things that are out of our control. We can't choose how people are going to treat us. Sometimes bad things do happen, no matter how hard we try to prevent them. But one constant that will always remain the same, one constant that we can rely on, is that we have the complete and total power and control over how we react to the world.

10 key principles of Stoicism

To help us get a better understanding of what a Stoic is like, and what principles are followed when it comes to this school of thought, we are going to take a look at the ten key beliefs that come with this. They include:

1. Live in agreement with nature and other things around you.

2. Live by virtue

3. Focus on what you are able to control, and then learn how to accept the things that you can't control.

4. Distinguish between good, bad, and indifferent things and adjust your reactions to those.

5. Take action. A true philosopher doesn't have to just sit back and let things happen. They are action takers and are even more effective because they are in control of which actions they use.

6. Practice misfortune. While Stoicism should be about learning to accept things you can't control, practicing a bit of misfortune can go a long way. it helps you to be prepared when things don't go your way, which can help you to really progress because these bad things won't take you by surprise.

7. Add in a reserve clause to all your planned actions. Think of this as your plan B. The more prepared you are, the less minor setbacks are going to aggravate you.

8. Love everything that happens. No, everything may not be perfect like you want, but it is all part of the bigger picture of your life. Learn how to accept and love

everything that happens to you, and you will get more richness out of life.

9. Turn all of your obstacles in life into opportunities. Often, perception is going to be key with this kind of philosophy.

10. Be mindful. Mindfulness is so important to getting the results that you want from Stoicism.

What does a Stoic look like?

The image that is usually out there about Stoics is that they are unemotional, unsympathetic, and that they don't really have feelings at all. While these people can remain calm in more situations than others, this doesn't mean that they don't have feelings. It simply means that they have found more effective ways to deal with their feelings. Instead of letting those feelings come out and make a scene or hurt someone else, they take control of the feelings and decide what will happen to them.

The misconception of an emotionless person comes from the idea that Stoics shouldn't allow themselves to be carried away by any unhealthy or irrational passions. Yes, they can feel these emotions, but they don't have to react to these emotions in a way that is unhealthy or will cause some harm to others. It is completely natural to feel these kinds of emotions, but that doesn't match with our rational human nature when we choose to act out just because we are having these emotions. There are going to be times when emotions start to take over. Someone says something mean to you, you feel sad when a situation occurs, you feel overly happy and excited about something. These are all things that happen in our lives, and the automatic emotions that stem from them are completely normal. We can't always control was is going on around us, no matter how hard we try, and letting go of that and working on what we can control (which, in this case, is how we react to our emotional response), can make the difference between a Stoic and a non-Stoic.

In many cases, a Stoic is going to try to use training and reason to help themselves not act out just because they are feeling things. They don't ignore the feeling. But instead of just letting the emotion take over, they take a step back. They acknowledge that the emotion is there. Ignoring the emotion can be even worse than letting it out and letting it have control. So, as a Stoic, don't forget the important part of recognizing the emotion that you are having.

But instead of reacting, you will look at that emotion and respond to it with virtue and reasoning. After taking a step back, you may realize that you are having an emotional reaction, but in reality, it doesn't match up to the situation. For example, have you ever had a situation where you exploded at someone over something that was really small and didn't mean anything? A Stoic is less likely to have these situations occur because they take a step back, look at the emotion and the situation, realize that acting out really isn't warranted in this case, and then finds another way to deal with the situation.

Think of how many disagreements and arguments could be avoided if everyone was able to do this? It isn't always easy. The easiest path is to just let the emotion out and not think about the actions until everything is done and over with. But to add more calm and reasoning to your life, and to really make yourself happier overall.

The Stoic is not going to be someone who doesn't have any feelings. They have the same feelings that anyone else does. But they have learned how not to be enslaved to these feelings. This is not the same thing as being insensitive or without feelings. It takes a lot of time and energy to learn how to be more self-disciplined and to have courage. They have the same feelings as before, but managing these emotions and getting them to behave the way that you want, rather than you behaving the way your emotions want, is the key to gaining true happiness.

Think about how many friendships you have ruined over the years because you reacted in anger or in frustration, and did things that you weren't proud of. How many feelings did you hurt along the way? How many people have you driven away with your rage, your sadness, or any of the other emotions that you have felt? If you have ever done something and then later regretted it, then you have, at least in part, allowed yourself to be controlled by your emotions, rather than being the one who controls their own emotions.

Now, it is fine to react to your emotions at some points. This is the beauty of how Stoicism works. Just because you are following this ideology doesn't mean that you have to let everything hit you and you can never show happiness, sadness, anger, or any other emotion ever again. But the key here is that you get to choose when to show those emotions. If you take a step back and find that the situation warrants one of those emotions, then go ahead and show it outwardly. In other cases, you may find that the emotion just doesn't fit with the situation, or you may decide that, even though the situation warrants anger or another emotion, it just isn't worth your time and energy to focus on that.

There are many ways that you will be able to describe a Stoic, and these will really help others to understand more about what is in this philosophy. Some of the statements that help to describe the personality of someone who is a Stoic will include:

1. They are confident and serene, no matter what comes their way. This does take some time and practice to master, so don't worry or get upset if you slip up on occasion.

2. They act based on reason rather than on emotions.

3. They focus on what they are able to control. And they don't worry about the things that they can't control.

4. They accept their fate, without whining or moaning, and you never hear them complain.

5. They are forgiving, generous, and kind. This often stems from the idea that they are able to control their emotions, and then they can take a look past their own issues and see the point of view of the other person in that situation.

6. The actions they take are prudent and they take responsibility for them.

7. They know how to remain calm, and have learned how to keep themselves from being attached to external things.

8. They are going to possess a lot of admirable traits including self-discipline, courage, benevolence, justice, and even practical wisdom.

9. They are able to live in a kind of harmony with everything that is around them. This harmony is going to extend into nature, to the rest of mankind, and to themselves.

While there are different ideas of what a Stoic is all about, many of these are misunderstandings of the whole philosophy. There are many benefits to this kind of ideology, and following it can lead you to inner peace, better relationships with others, and so much more. It takes time and some patience to learn how to keep those emotions under control, and as a beginner, you may slip up and let those emotions out. This doesn't mean that you are a bad person or that you have failed when it comes to Stoicism, it just means there is more work for improvement as you go on your journey.

Chapter 2: The History of Stoicism

Stoicism was formed in early Greece, by Zeno, around 300 B.C. The work stoicism comes from the Greek Stoa Poikile, which means "painted porch." At the time, this was a public space that was available outside where philosophers of Greece were able to gather together and spend time talking. Many theories were discussed here and many of those were then included in the initial development of stoicism.

Chrysippus was one of the earliest creators of the doctrine established with Stoicism, and he spent time expanding on these fundamentals in his own writing. His explanations of this early doctrine help to make Stoicism a very popular philosophical movement during his time, and even up to today. He is often given the credit of giving the ideology of Stoicism the acclaim and recognition that we know it has had throughout the years; all thanks to his publications at the time.

According to Chrysippus, everything that happens around us, including things in our lives and in nature, is going to be dependent on a specific cause. That is, if there is something bad that is going on in your life, there is going to be some root cause that led you to this fate. Nothing that occurs in life is going to happen without a sequential cause and effect. On the same note, he also believed that we each have a say and play a role in our final fate and that we hold all the power to change it. He believed that for an individual to have a free soul, humans needed to have a clear understanding of these patterns.

Up to that point, Greece had undergone many eras of philosophical thought, including skepticism and cynicism. Yes, besides their literal meanings in modern times, they were actually schools of thought that many followed in ancient Greece. On its own, you will find that Stoicism didn't really last very long in ancient Greece, but parts of it ended up influencing other types of philosophies and religion throughout the ages after that time.

While there were many ideas developed under the umbrella of Stoicism, the most important of these is that idea that we have complete power and control over our emotions, and the ability to overcome the most harmful and negative of emotions is the best key to living our best lives. If we give in to these emotions, we are likely to cause distraction and hurt in our paths. But if we can overcome those emotions, it is much easier to remain happy and to keep some of the close relationships that we rely on so much.

Training in this philosophy will focus on a mastering of emotions, which can give us the ability to react to the situations that occur to us in a logical and controlled manner. We each can have a life that is satisfying and productive, but first, we need to learn how to get rid of negative feelings and anger, and then replace those with more meaningful actions. Understanding that life does have its own ebb and flow, that we all have things that are positive, and things that are negative, happen to us, and the ability to look at those situations both good and bad in a neutral manner is at the core of Stoicism and its ethical view. Remember, it's not all about failure to react to those things. You still have to be a part of the world around you and emotions are going to show up, no matter how hard you try. Instead, a Stoic realizes that they have the power to choose a logical reaction to any problems they encounter, rather than leading the situation with an emotional charge. It is a small difference, but it can really transform our paths and makes our thinking patterns change.

For example, you may get in a situation where your car breaks down and you are on the highway. You have a choice about how you can react. Some people may get upset and focus on how inconvenient this is and how they will be late for work. They get so caught up in the issue that they assume this is the only way to react in that situation. But in this situation, you have lost control. Your emotions are in control and you probably look and sound like a fool getting upset over a situation that is beyond your control. This negativity is going to carry with you throughout the remainder of the day, and can really put a damper on how you feel.

You also have the choice to take a view that is more Stoic. The car stopped working and now you are on the side of the road, yes, but it isn't something that you could control, and it really has no impact on you as a person. Being late won't end the world, and while this can be an inconvenience, it won't take long before you are able to get on with the rest of your day. When you live in reason, it means that you need to have an understanding of where your place is in the universe, and why we are here. In Stoicism, the person needs to live within the laws of nature and then learn how suffering and negativity can sometimes be a part of our worldly existence. Choosing to passively accept this fact, and not letting it control us, can lead to a lot of happiness and contentment.

Another thing to realize here is that all things living in this world have been created equal and that this process is not just about ourselves. We need to respect and accept the virtue of others. We are not in this individually; we are all citizens of the world and can go through the same trials and issues, emotions and more as each other.

As you can see from this, Stoicism isn't just an ethical idea. It is a way to live your life. In essence, Stoicism is all about being in the present moment and understanding your part and your place in our universe. You get to learn how to control your life and control how much happiness you get to have from one day to the next. And having this control, though it takes a lot of time, dedication, and persistence, can be just the answer you were looking for when you got started with this ideology. There are a lot of great reasons to accept Stoicism and the ideas that come with it. While many people assume it is just a school of thought that includes being unemotional and not caring about other people, this is not the way of a Stoic. In fact, they often get along better with other people because they recognize the other point of view, rather than just concentrating on their own. They are masters of their own emotions and know how to change the things they can control while accepting the things that they can't.

Chapter 3: How to Become an Unbiased Thinker

The first thing we are going to explore when it comes to Stoicism is how to become an unbiased thinker. Humans have developed a somewhat bad habit of putting their emotions, and all emotional thoughts, before any logical thinking. One of the main parts of being a good Stoic is that you will process your emotions, but you will choose to react to them logically instead. The emotions are still there, and the Stoic still recognizes these emotions, but the power they have over the individual is minimized.

Being able to do this and operate in a mode of total fairness is a virtue that most people lack in our modern world. A true Stoic is able to work within the laws of nature around them, and the idea of going against that in order to gain emotional status and personal gains is just going to lead you to a lot of problems later on. While it is in human nature to act selfishly and in our own benefit, this is a trait that can derail even the best of people.

Being unbiased in the thoughts that you have can really provide you with the ability that you need to see all the possibilities that are presented to you. People who only focus on the solution to a problem without considering the feelings that they have about the issue or those who don't consider who the person supplying the idea is will make the best decisions. They are able to think objectively and will take everything into consideration, without worrying about how they feel about the situation, or even how they feel about the other person.

We all have those people we just don't get along with. They rub us the wrong way, annoy us, or have done something that has harmed us in the past. But just because we don't like them doesn't mean they don't have good ideas to consider. If you pick out a winning project at work just because it was submitted by someone you got along with and ignored a project just because it was submitted by someone you don't like, then you are missing out on a lot of great opportunities along the way.

The brain is something that we need to explore a little bit here. The brain is going to process stimuli through touch, sound, and sight and then will send out a response. The first time that you gain exposure to something, it can take longer to process that information and make sense of what is going on. But the more that you are exposed to that same stimuli, the brain is going to start building pathways that can process the information faster. It will lead you to the same conclusion that was reached before.

This makes things easier on the body and is a matter of convenience for the brain. It is why we can do many tasks without even thinking about them. The downside to this though is that it becomes very easy to develop some negative patterns of thought. If we always have a negative outlook in situations, those pathways are going to become very strong, and we will always give a negative response. When you want to become a Stoic, you need to learn how to override these original pathways and exchange them for something that is much more positive.

Let's look at an example of this. Let's say that most of the time, you start to get frustrated and angry when you run into some traffic on the way to work. This can be frustrating, but not really that big of a deal. You have trained your brain to automatically get angry and anxious when you see traffic. This is a negative thought pattern, but it is primarily driven by emotions. You feel worried or angry about being late for work. If you take that emotion away though, then the traffic jam is just a matter of slowed progress towards your intended destination. It is no longer frustrating.

A great way to work on your brain and get it to change to a more positive way is to learn how to change the attitude you have towards things going on around you. Many of us can place ourselves as the victim in any situation, but in most cases, we are completely in charge of what happens, and we just need to see that. If you don't like the way that a situation is going, it is up to you to make the change. For example, instead of being upset about the way that your career is going and lashing out at your coworkers, you could decide to find a career that is more rewarding and make a change.

Taking the right responsibility for your own viewpoint and your own emotions can really become a motivating factor to make changes to better your own life. If you want something to become more positive for you, then you need to start treating your day, as well as those around you, exactly how you imagined in your daydreams. If you would never have a daydream about being rude to others and only doing the bare minimum each day, then you shouldn't let this negativity get into your day to day life.

Being unbiased in your life is not always easy. Each new situation that comes up is a new chance for you to stop and think about whether you are reacting on logic, or on your emotions. In the beginning, you will just react automatically, without thinking. But you need to learn how to remove yourself from a situation so that you can change this.

For example, if you are feeling upset with your partner, you may think that placing blame, saying mean things, and lashing out may feel good in the moment. But where has this gotten you in your past? Probably nothing but regret. Acting on emotions can bring out more bad emotions, and you get stuck in a vicious cycle that you can't improve. If you can't control the emotions, then it may be time to remove yourself for a bit, allowing yourself to think through your emotions before you say anything.

After a break, you may realize that the situation is not that big of a deal. Maybe you overreacted to something. Maybe you aren't feeling well. And maybe you were tired or hungry and that caused you to act a certain way. During this time, also consider how the other person views that same situation. Maybe they meant to say something nice, or something they thought was innocent, and your overreaction has left them confused and hurt.

Being able to step away from your emotions and think through the way that you react to different situations can go a long way in helping you to feel your very best. It can help you have more control, have more understanding with other people around you, and so much more.

Chapter 4: The Importance of Fortitude and Self-Control

The next thing that we need to take a look at is the importance of fortitude and self-control. Understanding how to navigate your own emotional response to different situations can take some self-control. It is something that you have to consciously think through, rather than just hoping that it happens. You need to feel your emotions, process those emotions, set these emotions aside, and then act in a logical manner when it is all done. The requirement to do this is a strong mind, and most people are not born with this skill. It is something that can be developed with a lot of training and practice.

In many situations, the idea of self-control is going to be seen as the same thing as being able to resist temptation. For many, this could be related to controlling bad habits, or food and overeating sweets. In the case of this book, it is more about resisting the temptation to act out on your emotions. Since most emotional reactions are going to be seen as overreactions, it is definitely a win in your corner if you are able to resist them.

Self-control is something that needs to be learned. While you may find a few areas of your life where you are good at self-control, there are some areas where you need to work on. For example, you may have a lot of dedication and discipline when it comes to the work that you do, but then you fail when it comes to the types and amounts of foods that you eat.

It is possible to build up more self-control in the areas that you want, as long as you are willing to put in the hard work to do it. The first step to doing this is to set goals that you would like to meet. No matter where you want to improve in your life, having a final destination, and steps to get there, is crucial. Half the battle with this self-discipline is knowing what needs to be done. We often procrastinate and spin our wheels when we don't already have a good plan of action in place. Once we have a good plan in place, it is easier to make sense of the problem so we can work on the issue.

Let's say that you have set a goal to be an unbiased thinker. You would set that as the final goal, and then you can develop smaller goals to help you get to that result. You can set the steps at what you would like, but make them clear and concise, set up a deadline for meeting each one, and don't' give up until you get there.

When you go through this process, make sure that you focus your energy on one goal at a time. If you try to work on two or more goals, you are going to find it is really hard to reach any goal at all. What you focus on is going to grow and change with you, so pick the goal that is the most important for you, and stick with that one until it is complete. Once you do that, you will be able to add on a new goal that you want to reach.

Chapter 5: Using Stoicism to Become Free From Jealousy, Greed, and Anger

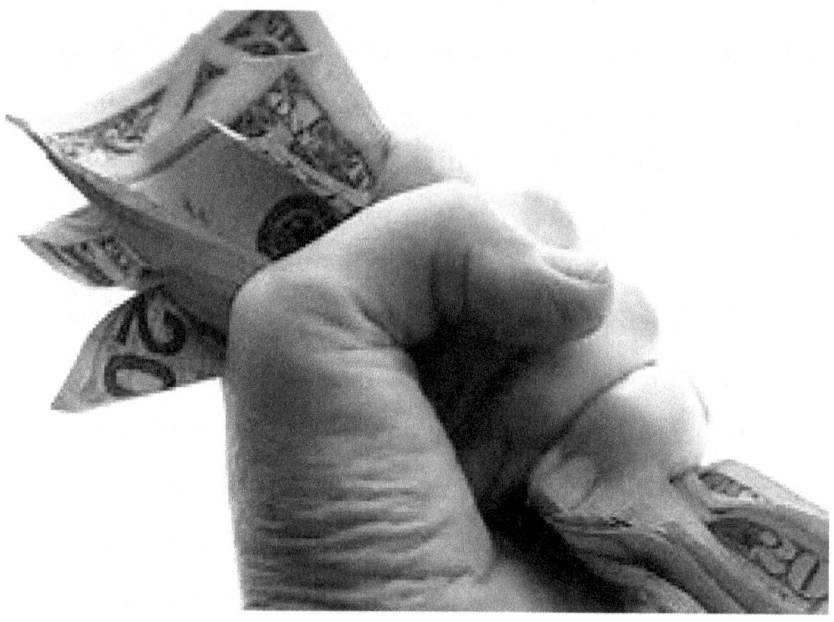

Once you have worked on having unbiased thinking and you improve your self-control and your fortitude, it is time to move on to using Stoicism in order to become free from anger, greed, and jealousy. These feelings are seen as some of the worst kinds of human traits. These feelings often stem from feelings of inadequacy in your own mind. Many times we let our minds get carried away and we may imagine things that are strange or aren't really there. In reality, the buildup in your head hardly ever carries through when you look at it in your real life.

For example, jealousy is a negative emotion that can often be found when you are in a personal relationship. A partner who is insecure may start fights with their significant other to make themselves feel better. In the minds of this person, they imagine that a small habit, like getting back home from work a bit late, are going to be because of infidelity or other bad things, rather than just running late because of traffic or working late at the office.

The response of picking a fight over something that is pretty much nothing is due to what made-up scenario you were building up in your own mind. You feel upset and angry over something that never actually happened, in anticipation that the action did happen. This can cause a lot of problems in a relationship because the one partner has let their imagination, and their emotions, get the better of them and upset them, and the other partner feels confused and hurt because they are being accused of doing something they never did.

Instead of giving your imagination time to wander, you should consciously decide to think about things that are more positive. In the example above, instead of imagining that your partner is late because they are cheating on you, think about all the more likely, and reasonable, options for why they are late. If this isn't working, make a quick call to your partner and figure out why they are running late.

On the other hand, always giving people the benefit of the doubt can be a bad thing as well. For example, if your partner is always coming home late from the office because they are cheating on you, it is still important to trust your instincts. You don't want to set up negative ideas in your head where problems don't actually exist, but you also want to listen to your intuition and listen to those emotions if they are telling you that something is up.

This is the beauty of Stoicism. You are able to still feel emotions. But you get to look at them logically and decide if they are actually true or not and how you want to react. If you feel that your imagination is just getting away from you, then you can choose to put those fears away and move on. But if you look at those emotions and feel that something is wrong, it may be time to investigate a little bit, and then decide where to act from there.

Freeing yourself from these emotions can really do a lot when it comes to improving your relationships and making sure that everyone involved gets a better quality of life. Getting to the bottom of what is triggering these emotions in you is really the best way to stop those emotions in their tracks. Remember here that you are not ignoring your emotions here; instead, you are going to process and then react to all the emotions that you have in a more rational way.

In fact, the more emotional intelligence that you have in your life, the easier it will be for you to become a Stoic. The goal here is for you to not suppress the emotions. It is fine to feel the emotions, but don't let them take control over your life. Learning what your emotional triggers are and taking time to really assess what is going on inside of you can help you to have more control over not only your emotions but also other aspects of your life as a Stoic.

Now we are going to do a little exercise. Was there ever a time when you felt angry and upset over something that seemed pretty small. But you still created a huge response, one that was overreacting for the situation. Was it really that smaller thing that had set you off from the beginning, or was there a bigger trigger that happened in the background that then influenced that reaction in the small issue?

For example, maybe one day you see that your spouse left some peanut butter on the counter when they were done with making a sandwich. Some days you walk by, put it back in the fridge, and that is the end of the story. But today, you get really angry and lash out. You aren't really angry about the peanut butter at this point. In fact, it may be because you had a bad day at work and feel underappreciated in your life. Or you may feel that it is a lack of care and consideration, one that you feel is a growing trend between the two of you in the relationship.

If you want to help yourself react in the proper way to situations around you, then you need to deal with the bigger and the original problem before it gets out of hand. This doesn't mean that you need to go through and rehash absolutely everything that occurred in your relationship since it first started. the better idea that you can work with is to point out things when they first come up. If you keep them bottled up inside, then it will be something small that will make you overreact to the situation.

And this is where Stoicism can come into play. When a situation occurs in your relationship that ends up making you mad or upset, then you will stop to think it through. You can decide if the issue is actually something to be upset about. If you think it is a big deal, you will talk to your partner about it right there and then. But if you decide that it is not a big deal, you will shrug it off and drop the topic right then and there. This can be something that is hard for a lot of people to do. They will hold onto their emotions and the things that make them mad. They don't want to rock the boat and make things difficult. But then they ignore the problems so much that everything explodes over something that is small and meaningless. Using Stoicism to decide how to deal with all situations can make a big difference in how you deal with each situation.

Dealing with the problem that is actually bugging you, before it has a chance to become a big deal, is the best option. If you run into issues with this, consider speaking with a trained counselor to help you sort out the different emotions that you are feeling. Many of us can make it through much of our lives without addressing some of the problems that we face, so figuring out the best way to get started can seem almost impossible. Asking for help can be hard as well, but they help you to dig through those feelings so you get a better understanding of where they come from, and you can rationalize them, and solve them better.

Even if you don't take the time to visit with a trained professional, make sure that you learn how to openly communicate with others. Holding things in and never expressing your views and concerns makes things difficult in several ways. First, if you keep them locked up inside, you are going to feel bad about yourself, and something tiny will set you off. And if you keep those emotions inside, no one knows where you stand in life, and that can make relationships hard. This communication can be helpful. The other people around you are not trying to cause you harm. They may not even realize that they are doing something that bothers you or something wrong until you let them know. They are too caught up in their own stuff that they don't realize that the actions they take are causing some issues and anger for others.

They don't mean this to be cruel to others; it is just the way that they got used to handling situations. Once you tell them that some actions are bugging them, they will be more than happy to make the changes. Just remember this communication is a two-way street and if they voice a concern with some of the actions that you do, be open and don't take them personally either.

This doesn't give you the right to criticize the other person endlessly. You can't be cruel about this. You need to open up the lines of communication and discuss your concerns with someone, but if you notice that they have had a bad day, or seem like something's going on with them, then maybe hold off your concerns. Don't bring up the concerns as a way to start a fight with the other person. Use it as a way to get your needs covered in a constructive manner.

Anger, greed, and jealousy can be the undoing of a lot of people and a lot of relationships. They are emotions that no one really wants to feel, because they can make us feel horrible and low. Learning when these emotions come up for us, how to avoid those emotions, and how you react to the emotions can really make a difference in how you feel and how healthy your relationships are. Stoicism is a great way to uncover the real reason that you are dealing with these emotions, and can help you to gain the control that you need over these negative emotions.

Chapter 6: How to Overcome Destructive Emotions

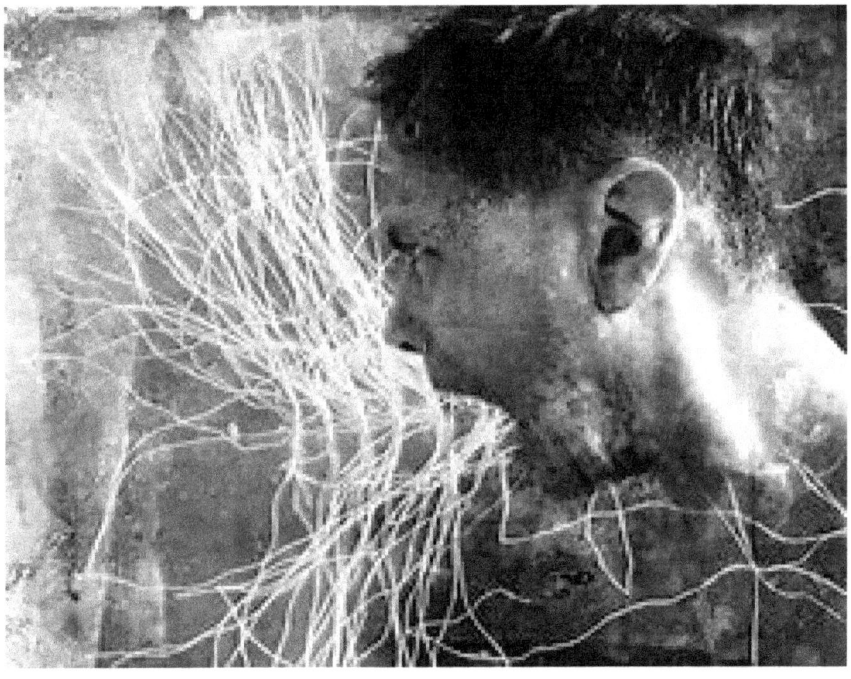

If you have ever allowed your emotions to take over the situation, you know how much this can get you into trouble. Those who have a short temper, even if it is only an occasional one, know that these overwhelming emotions can really cause them to act in a way that they are not proud of later on. They may say things that they don't mean, they may do actions they aren't happy with, and it can cause a lot of distrust and strain in every relationship.

In addition to causing issues with you and those around you, these feelings of anger and stress are going to affect your personal well-being. Jealousy and envy can often stem from feelings of inadequacy and low self-esteem. When we lack confidence in ourselves, we often have trouble controlling our emotions. We feel like we are out of control, we feel jealous of those who are confident in their own abilities, and all of this can cause us to feel angry.

When we feel in this manner, we continue to manifest even more anger, and more stress, that can be bad for us maintaining control, as well as for our health. Any emotion that causes us harm, and can cause to those around us, is destructive. But this is the reality that many people live with, and since they don't learn how to separate themselves from these emotions, they end up in a vicious cycle along the way. If you want to implement Stoicism into your life, then you must learn that these destructive emotions have no place in your life. Not only are bad emotions like greed, envy, jealousy, and anger destructive, but too much happiness can be a problem as well. How can happiness be a destructive emotion? If you are happy but it turns you into a person who is inconsiderate and careless towards others, then happiness can become bad as well.

For example, if you own your business and there are a few employees who work with you, you must make sure that all of the actions that you take aren't going to affect the business in a negative manner. Being very happy and excited, and never asking for input from your team and from others before taking a new direction in your business can turn your actions into destructive ones.

Since happy destruction emotions aren't as likely as the other ones that we talk about, we are going to skip over these in this guidebook and will spend more time focusing on the negative ones. These negative emotions can lead to a lot of anxiety, depression, and stress in your own life, which can manifest itself in the relationships that you have as well. As a Stoic, it is important for you to learn how to get out of the mire and oppression of these thoughts so that you can remain in control and live a happy and productive life at the same time.

This can seem hard to do. We live in a world where it is normal for people to hold onto their emotions, pressing them down deep and ignoring them. But this never works. All that suppressing the emotions does is cause you to blow up at some little thing, and takes the control of your emotions out of your own hands. Stoicism goes against these ideas, allowing you to express these emotions in a safe and effective manner where you get to be in control and decide what is the best time and place to let the emotions out, or even to decide that the situation doesn't warrant the reaction at all.

A good method that you can use to bring in some balance to your destructive emotions is to find positive things that can counteract them. Mindfulness can be used in this scenario. Learn how to be more aware of your surroundings, and concentrate on finding the good in life. Often we get too caught up in the negative things, the things that aren't going our way. But once we start looking for the good, it is amazing how much good will show up.

If you haven't already, starting daily meditation can be a good way to become more in touch and centered with the emotions that we have. Meditation allows you to take a breather from reality, to slow down and clear the mind, and it can basically make you wrap your arms around your feelings and thoughts with the goal of controlling and harnessing them. Even taking fifteen minutes during the day to sit alone in the quiet can do wonders to helping you when you first get started with Stoicism.

While you are doing your session of meditation, or even going through therapy if you choose that option, you should stop to focus on how your emotions have impacted your outside life. For example, if you are prone to bursts of anger, you can consider how they affect your job and those you work with, your relationships, and how successful you are in your life. Have you missed out on a lot of opportunities because of the attitude you have?

Many times, we assume that it is other people who are keeping us from success. We think that we miss out on things because someone doesn't like it, because life isn't fair, or because we have no control over the situation, but in reality, it is because those bursts of anger that you experience are turning you away from your coworkers and making it seem like you are not the right person for the job. The control is completely yours, you just need to learn how to deal with the anger and your other negative emotions to make this happen.

Being able to make the connections between this cause and effect is really at the heart of the Stoicism ideology. As the story goes, or the old adage, every action is going to have a reaction. Each and every step that you have taken in the past is a result of the one that came before it. When you begin to recognize these patterns, and then work with making the right changes whenever you see a problem, is a great way to use Stoicism as a way to have more confidence and personal growth overall.

This process is going to take some time. You need to learn more about yourself, learn how to negate destructive emotional patterns, and learn how to control those emotions so that you can live your life based on logic, rather than your emotions, as much as possible.

Chapter 7: How to Use Stoicism to Take On the Negativity In Your Life

Stoicism can even be used to help you attack the negative things that are going on in your life. Many times negativity can seem to follow us around. No one wants to deal with it, but it is really a part of life that we need to deal with. We may not get the job that we want, those bills come due on occasion, and bad things happen no matter how hard we try to avoid them. Stoicism helps us to deal with these negative situations. You can't always control the situations that occur to you, but you can control how you react to those situations.

One of the best ways that you can attack any negative situation that occurs in your life is to imagine them in reality. In reality, you know that negativity is going to occur, and it is something that you will need to address. While some self-help books talk about how to just strike all those bad thoughts out of your life, this usually doesn't work, and it doesn't stop the bad stuff from happening.

With the theory of Stoicism, we are taught to imagine and logically think through the worst-case scenario. While it isn't the point for you to dwell and worry about every single bad thing that can happen to you in your life, but it does ask you to be prepared for them. When you are prepared for the bad stuff, or the negative things, you won't be taken by surprise when they, are something lesser, happen, you can remain in control over your emotions.

If you are able to take all of the different emotions out of a bad situation before it can even happen, you will find that you are better equipped to deal with that situation when it does actually happen. For example, have you ever had a time when you thought you would lose your job because you made one little mistake? The sense of fear and dread about losing your job can be crippling. But this won't happen if you already thought about it and prepared for the worst. It's likely that you won't lose your job at all, so you kept all of the emotions out of the mix and the situation.

In the scenario above, what will happen if you do lose your job over that small mistake? Would you be able to find a job right away? Would you have the option to go back to school? Do you have enough money to rely on or could find something to tide you over for a few months? Thinking through this helps you to get through a plan in the unlikely case that you would be fired for that small mistake. And often, you will find that things will be just fine if you do get fired. This can make even the worst case scenario look like not a big deal, and you can get through the situation better without worrying about the emotions getting in the way.

The reality in life is, there are a lot of events that can happen to you throughout your life, but very few of them are going to be life-threatening. The car breaking down, something needing to be fixed on the house, losing your job, and more won't kill you and won't be the end of the world unless you let them. Taking the time before they happen to look at how you will react in those situations can make a big difference in how the situation pans out for you.

Chapter 8: How to Recognize Stoicism in Your Modern Life

For many people, the idea of practicing Stoicism seems impossible. They think that this is an old idea, one that can only work in ancient Greece. They may not understand how this philosophy works and decide that it is too hard for them to learn and implement into their own lives. Or they worry that they will become too distant and cold if they decide to go with Stoicism, so they write this school of thought off.

Even though times have changed since the beginnings of Stoicism, and we are no longer in ancient Greece, there are still the same human conditions present in today's world as there were in the past. We as humans continue to grapple with the same fundamental questions including:

- How can I overcome the fears I have in life?

- What is the best way that I can handle any success and failure in my life?

- Is it possible for me to be a good person and help others, while still being successful?

- Why am I so afraid of death?

- When I feel like my emotions are trying to take over, how do I deal with them?

- I want to live a life that is good, but what does that actually mean?

The fundamentals that come with Stoicism can still be used today. In fact, since the basis of this school of thought includes good reasoning and realism, they can be even more relevant today than ever before. It can help you learn how to love others better, how to bear negative emotions, and how to gain more control over your own life.

In Stoicism, you learn how things actually work, rather than putting your own ideas on things and wishing them to work out the way that you want. This is where a lot of frustrations and anger in our modern world stem from. We want to be able to control everything. We want everything and every minute of our lives to fit perfectly together, and then, when life ends up going the way that it wants, rather than the way that we want it too, we become very frustrated.

When you learn that you don't have control over everything, you can then make your choices on how you want to react, and on the things that you can actually control. So, if you are anxious because you are waiting for things that may not even stay or arrive, things may not go the way that we want. There may be certain things that we can do to make them better, but there is always a bit of uncertainty, and we need to accept that. Let's say that you want to have good health. You do have some control over some parts of your health. You can try to eat healthily and get plenty of exercise. You can make sure that you get outside and you spend time with others who are important to you. You can even go in for your yearly checkup to make sure that you are doing well. But still, there are going to be times when you will get sick, despite your best efforts. You may get sick less often than others, but you will still catch a cold or something along the way.

Getting upset about this fact is just going to make things worse. Everyone gets sick and worn down on occasion, and that is just a part of life. You can get upset and frustrated and lash out at people. Or you can just stock up your medicine cabinet, take a day off work to relax, and then move on with your day. Which one sounds like a better use of your time and effort and will make you feel happier in the end?

Another issue that Stoicism can help with is the idea of loneliness. When we look at this emotion from the viewpoint of a Stoic it is basically a feeling in need of any type of help that you lack. It is a type of helplessness that has been combined with a sense of isolation.

This isn't how most of the world sees the idea of loneliness. We think of this emotion as arising when we are away from people more than we want or when we have lost connection to a close tie (such as when a close friend moves away or we lose a loved one), or even when an individual has some anxiety about the quality of their ties. But the Stoic definition can be more useful. There are many times when we are alone without other people and don't feel lonely, so the traditional definition can't be the right way.

If you let the feeling of loneliness take over, you may have trouble even living your modern life. Let's say that you meet a widow who often starts to feel lonely near the end of March because it was her husband who did all of the taxes. As a Stoic, she wouldn't focus on that emotion, even though it is fine to miss the husband. She would realize that using a tax software or an accountant could get the bills done and could fill the basic need that has caused the loneliness.

The widow is going to feel lonely because you think of taxes as a chore that makes her unhappy, one that she does not want to do because she doesn't need the reminder that her husband is no longer there. The procrastination that she goes through demonstrates a fantasy that she would be able to bring her husband back by pretending he isn't there. She may understand that getting the job done is the best choice and would probably make her feel better but she is determined that it won't make her feel less lonely.

When it comes to some of the thornier problems that we have to deal with during our lives, the remedy is simply to accept things that you can't solve with your own actions, and learn how to avoid the extra unhappiness of longing for the solution or the person who would be able to solve it for you. You should also be wary of berating yourself in this situation because you haven't brought in the right problem solver to make things better. This just makes the situation worse in the long run.

Loneliness is just one of the issues that you may have to deal with when it comes to Stoicism in our modern world. You want to be able to deal with all of the negative emotions, including longing, loneliness, anxiety, and anger. You may only have one or two of these that are really bad in your life, but it is still important to take the time to learn how to handle these strong emotions and not let them take control over you. Overcoming these negative emotions is something that is going to take a lot of training. Think of mastering Stoicism like you would with mastering any other skill, such as a new instrument, doing something in math, or learning how to drive. You need to spend some time practicing and taking lessons, and you are going to make mistakes. But it does get better.

Stoicism can help you to find remedies for anger, and the other negative emotions, so that you are able to feel better and not have to worry about how they take control over your life. Let's take an example of anger. If you are dealing with anger on a regular basis, some of the steps that a Stoic may be able to use to help them deal with the anger and not let it take control over their lives will include the following:

1. Engage in some meditation ahead of time to help you feel calmer and not let anger take control.

2. Check anger as soon as the symptoms start to creep in. Never wait on this because anger can quickly get out of control.

3. Try to avoid people who make you angry and irritable, and instead focus on ones who are serene and easier to get along with. The Stoic mind will be able to figure out who will fit best with them.

4. Do some purposeful activity that can relax the mind and makes the stress and anger go away.

5. Find environments that you can spend your time in that have pleasing colors.

6. Don't try to engage in a deep conversation when you feel tired.

7. Don't engage in these same deep conversations when you feel hungry or thirsty.

8. Engage in cognitive distancing. This is basically when you learn how to delay your responses so that you can think through them and pick the right reactions for the situation.

This is just an example of how you can use a Stoic mind to help you deal with the anger that is going on. But you can employ these same steps if you are dealing with loneliness, frustration, sadness, or some other negative emotions. It is important to learn how to recognize those emotions and acknowledge that they are there. But from there, you can move on to thinking logically about how you want the situation to play out, how you want to look to other people, and so much more.

Chapter 9: The Stoic Methods to Helping Improve Your Modern Life

If you are looking for a guide that can help you keep all your sanity in our complicated and busy modern world, then Stoicism is the right choice for you. You may wonder why you would want to follow a school of thought that comes from the ancient Greeks, but anyone who has tried it out in the past and implemented it into their lives has found that it can be a great way for them to improve their lives, get a handle on their emotions, and so much more. Our modern world, perhaps more than any other time in history, really needs a steady framework to help them set priorities, orient themselves, and learn how to appreciate all the good in their life while handling all the bad.

While the ideas of Stoicism may seem complicated or like it is too old and ancient to apply to our modern lives. But in many ways, when you start to add these principles into your life on a daily basis, you will be surprised at how liberating it can feel. When it comes to adding more Stoicism to your life, there are going to be four main virtues that are very important to seeing results. These include:

- Practical wisdom: This is the knowledge of what is bad and what is good, and what needs to be done in both cases.

- Courage: This isn't just talking about physical courage. It also is going to talk about moral courage or the courage that you need to face all of your challenges each day with integrity and clarity.

- Temperance: This is going to be the exercise of moderation and self-restraint in all the different aspects of your life.

- Justice: This is where you will work on treating others fairly, even if they have done you wrong.

At the base of this philosophy is the idea to respect other humans. The ancient Stoics were the only group of free people at that time who openly opposed slavery and who considered women to have the same rights as men. With that said, it is a great ideology to implement into your own life any time that you want to make improvements, or when you see that things just seem to be overwhelming to handle on your own.

In this chapter, we are going to take a look at some common modern challenges that many people tend to face, as well as the approach that you would use as a Stoic to help you handle that situation. As you go through, you will quickly see that this is a great method to add to your own life, that it is simple, and you will see results in no time.

I'm under stress all the time

Despite what it may feel sometimes, stress is not something that is placed on you. Often it becomes a part of your life because you have expectations that are misguided, you are attached to certain outcomes occurring, or you try to control things throughout your life that you can't control.

Let's say that you would like to finish getting a room prepared for your aging parents to move into, but you weren't able to get it done by the deadline that you implemented on yourself. You should accept that, rather than getting mad and wallowing in regret. Remember that you aren't able to always control the outcomes of situations. But you can also turn this into a good learning experience for setting more realistic expectations next time.

A practice that you can try out when you want to deal with this problem is to get out a journal and write out the answers to three important questions. These questions are - What could I have done differently today? What were some of the things that I did right today? What did I do wrong today?

I have demands that are really relentless on my time

A Stoic is often going to realize that their time is a very precious resource. And they refuse to easily give it away since they can never get that time back. They also know that they shouldn't fritter away their time on things that are not worth it. As a Stoic, it is important to learn when you should say no to people, especially when it is not something you want to do or something that you are comfortable with giving away.

In the same idea, make sure that you aren't stealing time away from the people who really do matter to you. Yes, you may have five hours available after work, but giving 4 away to one person may mean that you miss out on time with your family or those you love the most. As a Stoic, you need to place a strong emphasis on responsibility to your family so time taken from them is never a good thing and they avoid it as much as possible.

I end up spending a lot of time online, and then I feel bad

As a Stoic, you recognize that technology isn't a bad thing, but it isn't always a good thing either. The way that you use this technology is what is really under your control, and can help make you a better person. You don't have to give up technology and online time just because you are a Stoic. But if you are wasting time online, spreading gossip online, and using that instead of spending time with your family, then there is something wrong with the technology.

If you use your Stoic training in the proper way, you will find that digital technology can be like a virtue gym. It gives you a lot of opportunities to exercise your character and your ethics. When people say things that are mean to you or aggressive, you can choose to not respond to the issue. You can delete the post or unfollow instead if you can't ignore it, but avoiding a big confrontation can be the best way to make sure that you maintain your control over the situation without letting it get the best of you.

Even though I'm not doing horrible financially, I never feel content with my possessions and wealth

This is a big problem that many people in the modern world feel. They may make a good income, but we are often bombarded with a lot of advertisements and other media that show us glamorous lives. We see all the things that other people have, and we feel like we are falling behind. This emotion of envy and jealousy can rear its ugly head and make it very difficult to be happy with the things that we already have.

There is nothing about the ideology of Stoicism that says that wealth is bad or that you can't have wealth and use it to have a good life. The ancient Stoics came from all walks of life. Some were slaves and some were very rich. There is nothing wrong with money or having money, but Stoicism often sees it as a great temptation if you don't know how to use it properly. The more people have of wealth, the more they are going to focus on expensive experiences and possessions, and the more they will want.

How do you get yourself out of this endless cycle of getting more money, and then always wanting more? First, you need to recognize that possessions are just external objects, things that you can lose. Yes, they are nice to have and you are lucky to own them, but it is possible that your luck will turn at any moment, and then all those things will be gone.

Now, this is the worst case scenario, losing all your possessions. Now that you have been able to mentally accept this outcome, which is unlikely, you can learn how to change your mindset about the things that you own. If you run into issues with this one, you may want to try "practicing" not having things for a bit. This helps them to get used to the idea that everything they have is going to be borrowed from the universe, and you are lucky to have them.

When we learn how to appreciate the things that we have more, and we see them as gifts from the universe, some of that longing for more wealth, for more possessions, will go away. Sometimes it is all about removing some emotions, like envy and jealousy, from the situation to help you to appreciate what you have and keep yourself from worrying about material things.

As I age, I always feel worried about the health I have

All of us have health conditions when we get older, no matter how well we take care of ourselves along the way. While there are a few things that you can do to help improve your health, such as eating healthy, getting some social interactions rather than being isolated, visiting the doctor, and being physically active, aging can catch up with you. You can reduce the severity of it, but you will notice a difference between your 60-year-old body and your 40-year-old body.

In this scenario, it is important to recognize what you can control, and what you are not able to control. You should also learn how to let go of the desire to control outcomes in your life because these are definitely out of your control. You can avoid bad stuff, eat right, and exercise, and make the right medical decisions all day long, but you are still going to get sick on occasion, and you can't always control the outcome of that illness.

In a sense, when you worry too much about yourself and whether or not you will get sick, you are participating in a form of narcissism, an attitude that Stoics will want to avoid. You are able to avoid this by simply recognizing yourself about your place in space and time. in a world where focusing on yourself is seen as completely normal, this can take some time. and it isn't an invitation to forget about yourself and never take care of yourself. But it is a way for you to learn how to let go of various things, like getting a cold, that you aren't able to control.

I feel fear when I think about dying

No matter how scary it may seem to some people, death is natural, and it is something that is going to happen to everyone. We must accept this, or it is impossible to be truly happy as you live your life. If you are constantly fearing death and being worried about it, how are you supposed to enjoy the life that you have? You can't control death. It is going to come at any time and manner that it wants no matter what you have to say about it, and trying to force it to behave in any other way is futile. Accepting death and the afterlife can be a good way to find true happiness.

Part of accepting death is to prepare for it, but this is definitely not something that Americans work on. They never put together a will, they do not worry about a power of attorney, and they never put out a do not resuscitate order. This can make it very hard at the end of your life, both for you and for those who have to take care of you.

Stoics consider it a very courageous thing to prepare for death and the end of life, and it is a refreshing exercise. This exercise forces you to get through your fears, your anxiety, and even your anger so that you think in a rational manner. According to even the most ancient Stoics, the biggest test of character is how one handles the last moments of their life. Prepare for your end of life ahead of time, face your fears, and you will soon see how being a Stoic can benefit your life.

The examples that we discussed above are great ways to show how Stoicism, even though it is an ancient philosophy, can be used in our modern world. More than ever, our modern world has left people emotional, out of control, stressed out, and not sure what to do. Implementing the Stoic philosophy into your life and trying to follow it as much as possible may be the answer that you need to help solve many of the major problems you face today. Once you get past the misconception that Stoicism is all about being cold and heartless, you will see that it is actually a great approach that can help you to improve your life and see great benefits.

Chapter 10: Why Should I Implement Stoicism in My Life?

This guidebook has taken some time to talk about the various parts of Stoicism. We looked at the main principles that come with this ancient school of thought, why it is so important to the different parts of your life, and even some ideas on how you can start to implement it today. But now it is time to take a look at some of the basics of why you should implement Stoicism into your life, and the basics of why it can make great improvements in your life, even in our modern life.

Helps you build better relationships

One of the best benefits that you will be able to get when you get started with Stoicism is that it helps you to have better relationships with everyone around you. You get the benefit of having a better relationship with your family, with friends, with co-workers, and with other people you encounter each day. It may take some time to accomplish, but if you work at it, you are going to see a huge improvement in your overall quality of life and the types of relationships that you get to enjoy.

Think of how hard it is for other people to be around you. When you explode over little things or get too emotional and can't stop because the emotions have started to take over, you can be very unpredictable and hard to get along with. You may drive a lot of people away from you, people who don't really want to deal with all the emotions, or who were hurt along the way and decided to give up.

With Stoicism, you can change this. You can get in control of those emotions and tell them when you want them to come out. This doesn't mean that you aren't allowed to have any emotions at all. It simply means that you need to take a step back from the emotions, think about those emotions in an objective manner, decide if the situation warrants those emotions at all. If the situation does warrant the emotion, then you can express it. If the situation doesn't warrant that emotion, then you need to learn to just let it go and move on.

Helps you to not sweat the little things

Often the things that are the smallest are the ones that get us worked up the most. A glass left on the counter is a small deal, but many times we let it blow out of proportion and then get into a fight because that glass was left out. We worry about being a few minutes late to school. We worry about what we are wearing and if anyone will think that it looks bad. We worry about a million little things, and we let these things take over our lives, but none of them are really worth the effort. With Stoicism, we start to take a look at our lives and our actions and make conscious decisions on how we want to react to things. We learn to let go of all the little things that we can't control. If you are late for work because you leave the house too late, then make a change and leave home a few minutes early. But if you are late for work once because there was an accident on the road that stopped all traffic, then just let it go. You will be surprised at how many little things you hold onto and make into big deals once you start looking into them. Allowing these little things to control your emotions and cause problems is really not worth it. Use Stoicism to help you let go of the little things, to keep your emotions in check, and see how well your happiness can grow over time.

Helps you to be in more control over your life

Do you ever feel that you are losing out on the control that you want in your life? Do you feel that others get to make the decisions for you, or that your emotions are ruining all of your relationships? Then it is time to make some changes and Stoicism can make the results that you would like.

If your emotions have control over your life, it becomes really hard for you to get the things that you want. If a little bit of anger can make you overreact and then you do or say something that you don't mean, this can be really damaging in many aspects of your life. If these anger emotions cause you to be mean and say bad things to your partner, then you may find that they get tired and they leave. If you let these emotions come out when you are at work or other social situations, you could make it hard to make friends, to get along with others, and even keep your job.

When you start to implement the ideas of Stoicism into your own life, you will find that it is easier to get this control back.

Remember that Stoicism doesn't mean that you have to be devoid of emotions. It just means that you decide when and how to use those emotions. If you take a look at an emotion and decide that it isn't the right one for that situation, or you decide that you don't want to waste your time on that emotion, then you will move on and handle the situation in a different way.

In some cases though, you may decide that it is best to let the emotion out. Stoics do feel anger at some points. But instead of letting it turn into all-out rage and letting it ruin how they interact with others, they use that anger to help tell someone what is bothering them or even to effect change in the world. A Stoic can easily be happy and joyous about something, but they learn how to manage it so that the emotion doesn't take over and make them into something bad. In Stoicism, there is even room for the other emotions, the Stoic is just more in control of them and can make the big decisions on when and how to use those emotions.

Can help you handle stress better

How many times do you feel the stress creep up on you? You feel that you are overwhelmed by what is going on in your life, you may want to scream and get angry, your neck muscles tighten and you may even catch your hands in a fist by your sides. Stress can cause so many issues to the body, such as an elevated heart rate, health conditions, headaches, and so much more. But despite these issues, you will find that most

Americans are dealing with stress, at least part-time, and can't seem to make it go away.

Stress is often going to be a side effect of not being able to control what is going on around you. You want to have control, but you find that some things are just not going to work the way that you would like. In addition, it could be a result of issues of not being able to manage your time and say no to things that don't really mean much to you (such as helping out at work more when you'd rather spend time with your family), which can make us feel very stressful.

Stoicism can help you to deal with the stress in your life. You learn how to recognize the emotions that are going on in your mind, and then you can make decisions based on what will make you the happiest and will ensure that you get what you want out of life. When you can make smart decisions that make your life easier, and when you learn to let go of the things that you have no control over, you will find that the stress starts to go away.

Helps you to live in the present moment

How many times do you focus your energy on thinking about what happened in the past, or what is going to happen in the future? Now compare that time to how much time you actually spend concentrating on the here and now, the things that actually matter at this point in life. Often, the latter is only going to happen when a big, significant thing happens in our lives, but as a result, we are missing out on so much that can be amazing.

Stop focusing so much on the past and the future. You can't do anything about what happened in the past, and until someone creates a time machine and you can use it to go back, you just have to live with what occurred. And while you can make different decisions to help influence the future, you can't have full control over what is going to happen to you in the future either. So why get so worked up and worried about it, and why spend so much of your time focusing on it, when you could just focus your energy on the here and now and see some great results instead.

Helps you to stop caring what others think about you

It has happened to all of us. We worry about the way that others perceive us. We dress up a certain way because we think that it is important to have a certain appearance to different events. We worry that when we mess up, others are going to think lower of us and make fun of us, and this can cause a whole host of other issues along the way.

With Stoicism, you can learn how to not worry about these things as much. It may be hard. We live in a society where appearances seem to matter more than they should, and we all want to live up to an impossible standard that the celebrities like to shove on us. But this is not the way that most people live, and neither should you. It just adds in stress, brings out our own insecurities, and so much more.

Stoicism can help us to take a step back and not focus on what others think so much. Instead, you will learn more about how to take a step back, figure out why your appearance towards others is so important, and then make the changes necessary to free yourself from that idea and just enjoy life instead.

Learn how to be thankful for what you have

Often our emotions can make us feel ungrateful or sad about the things that we have. We may have a nice place to live, food on the table, and so much more, but we still feel like we are missing out or like we don't have the same things or quality of life that others do. This can make it hard to feel happy, and those feelings of anger, jealousy, and envy just keep getting worse.

When we are able to implement the ideas of Stoicism into our lives a bit more, we find that it is easier to be thankful for what we have. When we see that someone else has something nice, or something that we want. We can choose not to react and then take a step back and see all of the good things that we do have. And once we take a close look at all the blessings that we already have, it becomes a lot easier to be thankful.

Implementing Stoicism into your life is not always going to be easy. Humans can be very emotional creatures and turning those emotions off, or at least being able to control them and think about them critically is not something that we are used to. But the tips and tricks in this guidebook are there to help you along the way and will give you the guidance and help that is needed to really see Stoicism work for your needs.

Chapter 11: Is It Possible to Become Too Stoic?

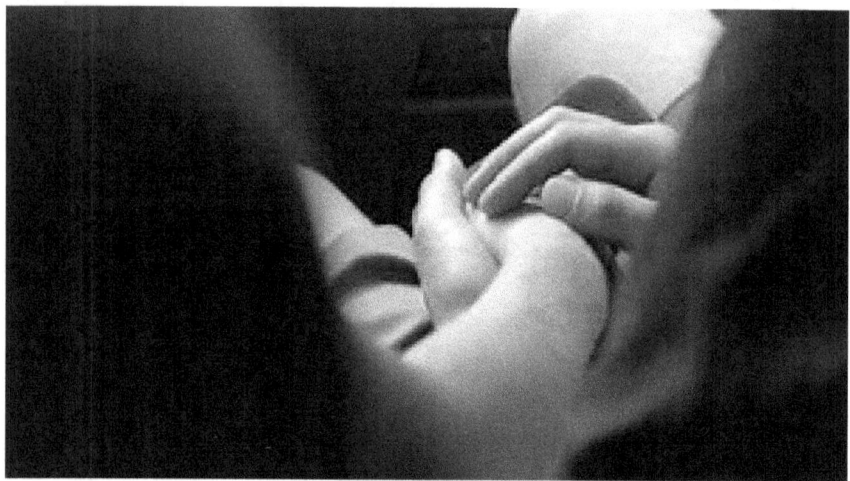

The next question that you may have about the ideology of Stoicism is whether it is possible to be an extreme Stoic? Is it possible to take this idea too far and become so Stoic that no one wants to be around you? If you are following the principles that the found fathers had with Stoicism, it isn't possible to take this to the extreme. With that said, Stoicism can sometimes be used in the improper manner and this has given it a rap as an emotionless existence where the person is overtly logical and cold and doesn't take the feelings of the other person into consideration.

When it comes to Stoicism, you will find that it can be the perfect combination of compassion and logic. You can still feel your emotions, you can still feel the plight of someone else, respect their boundaries, and the laws of nature and this earth, and still make decisions that are logical and ones that don't have emotions that control or drive them. While this doesn't seem like it to someone who hasn't practiced Stoicism, the emotions actually are a big part of the decision making process. You just decide in a logical manner if you are going to let the emotions play a part in your reaction or not.

Let's say that you are thinking about switching jobs. There are some benefits that come with working at your current job including a company car and a good benefits package that you already enjoy. Based on the idea of financial security, you really don't have a good case for leaving this position. However, in return for these benefits, you have a lot of long hours and stress for being there, and you feel pretty drained each day. This can negatively affect your relationships and even your ability to find some joy in life.

In many cases, an individual, even a Stoic one, would decide to leave their secure job and go for the other one if it had a decent pay, had good benefits, and promised fewer hours so they could enjoy life. These may not seem like logical choices when looking at finances, but the emotional considerations came into place with this decision.

If the Stoic were only about the logic of tangible things, such as their income, there would be one solution; stay where you are. But no one is able to ignore their emotions completely. In fact, feelings and emotions, specifically the stress response, are the way the body tells you that something is off and that you need to make some changes to your situation. Emotions don't have to be ignored in any situation, but you need to really consider them when making decisions, rather than letting them take over and control you.

Even as a Stoic, your decisions will be a balance of logical and emotional reason. A good compromise to work with would be to stick it out at the first job while looking around for a new place to work. This means that you are able to still receive your income and your benefits until you find something else that you will enjoy better.

If you start to lose connections with others, then you know that you have taken the idea of Stoicism too far. Thinking too logically means that you are going to take too much time away from some of the simple things that you should enjoy in life. And being too logical can make you seem cold and unsympathetic to those around you, driving relationships away. Stoicism should be a way to improve your relationships, not drive others away. If you feel that people are being driven away by the way that you act, then it is time to make some adjustments to what you are doing with Stoicism.

Chapter 12: How to use Stoicism for the Long Term and Planning Your Future as a Stoic

If you decided that it was time to add Stoicism into your life starting tomorrow, where would be the best place to start? There isn't really a clear starting point, because, like any other philosophy, the path isn't straightforward all the time. your best bet is to learn as much about Stoicism as possible, and then build up from there. Learning new concepts can take some practice, and experimenting with Stoicism a bit and see how it works for you.

Going from an emotional disaster, like many of us, over to a Stoic can be a big adjustment for the brain. You need to actually go through and rewire the way that it thinks. The more you start to hear about Stoicism, the more that you surround yourself with the ideas that come with Stoicism, and the more that you are able to expose yourself to Stoicism, the easier it is to rewire the brain to behave the way that you want. Even starting out by doing some meditation can make a big difference in how you view the world, how much you can control your anger, and how much you can implement Stoicism into your life.

During this time of education, make a point to put the words that strike you the most into action. If there are some ideas or passages that seem to hit home for you, make sure to add it over to your moral catalog. If you like the idea of gaining control over your emotions, then work on that. If you like the idea of letting go of things that you can't control, then focus your energy on that.

As you learn more about Stoicism, talk to others who use Stoicism, and just get more familiar with Stoicism, you are going to find a lot of things that really strike your interest. Keep these close, and when things get tough, make sure to remind yourself of them. Remember that just hearing these words on a regular basis can be enough to retrain the brain to a new way of thinking. Write the ideas down and then look them over on occasion, and see the difference they can make in your life.

But your whole process into Stoicism shouldn't just be about reading and writing things down the whole time. You need to actually get to work and do some actions to get the benefits of Stoicism in your life. You need to consciously monitor your emotions throughout the day. This isn't going to happen on its own. The brain wants to keep up with its traditional habits and ways of thinking. You have to actually go through and think about your emotions and what you want to happen rather than just letting those emotions happen.

For example, let's say that you are feeling upset or anxious. You can take some time to sit with those thoughts, without reacting, and figure out what is causing them to come in the first place. What you may not realize here is that your emotions are going to have a direct connection from the brain to the body. When our stomach feels like it is in knots, this is often the brain trying to signal to us that something isn't right at that time. If you can figure out what is causing those feelings, then it is easier for you to make them go away. Another thing that you can work on when you get started with Stoicism is to not sweat the little things. So many times, the things that really seem to make us the most upset are going to be the littlest things, the ones that don't really matter all that much. The next time that you get stuck in traffic, or you have to listen to your boss drone on during a meeting, allow the emotions to show up, but then invite them to just pass over you.

Yes, at times you are going to feel angry or annoyed at the situation, but these moments are going to pass. Allow yourself to notice the feeling, but then actively decide that you aren't going to assign a value to it at all, and you are not going to react, until the mind has had some turn going over the information.

Again, one of the best things that you can do when you first start with Stoicism, especially if you are prone to lots of anger and stress and frustration, includes meditation. There are many different methods of meditation that you can try out, and all of them can provide you with great results. The goal here, no matter which form of meditation you decide to go with, is to help you learn more about your inner self, to take a break from life, and start to realize that the little things don't matter that much.

You only need to take about fifteen minutes a day, either right away in the morning or right before going to bed. This is enough time to get yourself to calm down, to clear the head, and help you to get in control of what you are feeling. Explore a few different types of meditation, and try a few of them out, to figure out which one you like and want to stick with.

Using Stoicism to plan out your future

Planning your future can be a scary endeavor for some people. They worry that they won't have enough money to pay the bills. They worry that something bad will happen. But most people are just scared about the things that they can't control that may find them when they think about the future. But when you spend all your time being consumed with fear about the future,

Although fate is going to play some role in how your life turns out, your ultimate level of happiness is going to depend on you. This is your chance to make the most out of your life. This may mean that you will need to make some large changes in your life, or it could be as simple as rearranging how you view what is already going on in your life. Before you make the big changes though, explore making some small rearrangements to help you do this in the most effective manner.

For example, when you look at your life, do you see that it is really all that undesirable, or are you just unappreciative or selfish about what you already have in your life? If you find that you are just being selfish, then the only thing that you need to do is learn how to control your thinking and your emotional state, and things will get better. If you look around and notice that your life really isn't desirable, then it is time to make some big changes to your life to add in some more happiness.

If you decide that it is time to make some big changes in your life, then it is time to figure out what you want to do so you can make a plan. Ask yourself some questions like "What could I be doing to live a life that is more fulfilling? What am I doing now that makes me happy? What am I doing to bring meaning to the lives of others?"

While these questions may seem a bit vague in some cases, that is kind of the point. Each of us needs to explore these questions on our own and figure out the answers. Each person is going to come up with different answers and they are likely to change. But it is up to you to figure out the answers to all of these and then come up with the plan that will progress you forward.

At this point, you may be at a loss for how you can get started in Stoicism, and how you can create a plan for improving your own life. Here are some concrete tasks that you can think about to help this plan get started. first, pick out a tangible goal that you want to meet, and then write it down. Stick it along with some of your favorite quotes from Stoicism and leave them in a place where you can find them easily.

Let's say that you had a great idea of going back to school in order to study art. This is something that you always wanted to do, but you listened to your logical mind and went into a career that had more money and more stability. But your current career didn't really help to fill your soul. So, now you are ready to go back to art school and see how that can go for you.

At this point, the question is, how will you do this? Where will you go to school? Will you need help financing the school? How much time can you devote to this? Will you continue working while going to school and how will this affect your overall plan? Do you want to do this on the side or would you want to do this as a full-time career?

Think about all of the little steps that you will need to take in order to help you reach these goals. Then make sure to write these down. Once you have all the different steps in place, you can break them into tiny steps to give you a clear map. Remember that a Stoic mind is often going to be a logical one. It is fine to follow some of the passions that you have in life, but if you just jump in because of the emotions, without thinking through the consequences or the plan of attack, then you are not working as a Stoic. Writing all of this down as a thought-out plan can really help you to make sure you do this the right way.

During this whole process, you may feel like you are being overwhelmed with all of the small details and the hard work that is needed to reach the finish line. You may even start to feel a bit of anxiety and fear as you start to build up your map. This is yet another place where Stoicism can come into play as well. Use the skills that you have learned with Stoicism to take a step back and sit with your emotions.

Think about what is actually causing these emotions. Are you afraid of all the work that you have to do to make it to your goal? Are you scared that you are going to fail? As you are thinking over this goal, think about what the worst case scenario is going to be if you didn't get your art degree? If you have a plan put into place, it's likely that the worst thing you are going to have to deal with is that you stay with your current job and can't pursue your passions. This can be hard, but at least you still have stability and a job, and you can come back and try something else later on.

The motivation to really work on some changes in your life, and to focus on the things that make you happy can be the root of Stoicism. While it does ask you to think through your emotions and have a plan of attack when you are ready to handle any situation out of your control, these can be used to help you see the success that you want out of life. For some people, this can be hard to do. They want to follow their emotions because it is easy, but as we saw in the example above shows that you can listen to your emotions, but you will still use your logical side to help you finish that decision.

You can use these same ideas when it comes to any major decision that you want to follow. Think about the thing that is going to make the biggest difference in your life. What is going to make you happy in the here and now? Once you have that down (and it can be influenced by your emotions), you can use your Stoic mind to come up with a logical plan to actually reach the results that you want for success.

Now that you have given yourself a pep talk, it is time to go through that list that you have made, crossing off the tasks until you have gotten to the goal. Keep the big picture in mind the whole time. And when you actually reach the goal, you will find that you are doing something that you truly love, something that helps you make a good contribution to your community, and you get the benefit of enjoying the fruits of your labor along the way as well.

Planning your future can be tough. There are so many variables that come into play, but often the major reason that we won't sit and think about our future is that we are afraid of what will happen. Yet again, we have decided to let emotions get in the way of our own happiness, and have turned away from using logical thinking to improve our lives. When you start to work more with Stoicism and implementing it into your life with the tools that we discuss in this guidebook, you will find that it can make some great improvements to your future, and can plan out your future much better than you could ever have imagined.

Conclusion

Thank you for making it through to the end of *Stoicism*. Let's hope it was informative and able to provide you with all of the tools you need to achieve your goals whatever they may be.

The next step is to find ways that you are able to implement Stoicism into your own life. Many people have the wrong idea about Stoicism. They think that in order to be a Stoic or follow any of the ideas that come with Stoicism, you need to be void of emotions, cold, and lack sympathy for other people. But, as we explored through this guidebook, Stoics aren't missing out on emotions, they just know how to have emotions without worrying about how those emotions are going to take control over them.

Living a life of Stoicism is a great option to work with. You can take an evaluation of all the emotions you have, and choose whether you would like to express them or take a lot of route. This gives you a ton of freedom, can improve your relationships, helps you get further in life, and is one of the best ways to improve your quality of life.

When you are ready to learn more about Stoicism and how it can benefit your life, make sure to take a look through this guidebook to help you get started.

Finally, if you found this book useful in any way, a review is always appreciated!

Description

Are you looking for a way to improve your life? Do you feel that situations are often out of your control and you feel angry and frustrated that you can't seem to do anything about that? Are you constantly feeling bad for your actions when you get upset or angry, but you can't seem to control the emotions that take over you at times?

If these all sound like things that happen to you, then Stoicism may be the right choice. Stoicism is a way to take more control over your life. It ensures that you are going to be the one who controls your emotions. You still feel emotions, but you learn how to take a step back from those emotions and evaluate them. Sometimes, those emotions are warranted and you can let them out. But many times, those emotions aren't worth the effort or aren't merited for that situation, and you let them pass.

This guidebook is going to take some time to talk more about Stoicism, how it can benefit your life, and different ways that you can implement it. Some of the things that we will discuss in this guidebook include:

- What is Stoicism?

- The history of Stoicism and how it has changed throughout the years.

- How to become an unbiased thinker

- The importance of fortitude and self-control

- How to use Stoicism to become free from negative emotions like anger, greed, and jealousy.

- How to overcome some of the most destructive emotions that we feel.

- How to use Stoicism to take on the negativity that creeps into your life.

- How to recognize Stoicism in our modern world and in your own life.

- The reasons that you should implement Stoicism in your own life.

- Is it possible to become too stoic in your life?

- How to use Stoicism for the long term and how to plan your future as a Stoic to get the best results.

When you are ready to start implementing Stoicism into your own life, make sure to read through this guidebook to help you get the most out of this school of thought and philosophy.

Photographic Memory:

10 Steps to remember Anything Superfast! Accelerated Learning for Unlimited Memory Efficiency. Create Habits to Help You Improve Your Memory, Focus and Clarity. Mind Hacking!

Table of Contents

Introduction...85
Chapter 1: What is Photographic Memory?.................87
Chapter 2: Eating for Better Memory........................92
Chapter 3: Exercise Your Way to Improved Recall.......99
Chapter 4: Catch Some Zzzzzzz's!............................102
Chapter 5: Memorable Meditation............................106
Chapter 6: The Art and Science of Being Mindful.......113
Chapter 7: A Busy Mind Remembers More!...............120
Chapter 8: Time for Some Creative Thinking.............125
Chapter 9: The Power of Emotional Recall................133
Chapter 10: Small Tips and Tricks for Training Your Memory..141
Chapter 11: Becoming a Memory Champion..............146
Conclusion...157

Introduction

Congratulations on downloading *Photographic Memory: 10 Steps to Remember Anything Superfast,* and thank you for doing so. If you are interested in supercharging your memorization abilities, you have come to the right place!

There is a lot of conflicting and downright confusing information out there about how memory works, whether or not a photographic memory is possible, and how to train your brain to reach peak memory performance. This handy guide consolidates and explains every step that is necessary to train your memory to maximum efficiency. You will start by learning a bit about how the memory works and what it means to have a photographic memory. Next, we will dive into the steps towards optimizing your recall abilities.

Quite a bit of maximizing your memory potential depends on reaching optimum brain health, so we will teach you how to eat, exercise and sleep for a healthy brain. Next, you will learn about the critical links between mindfulness, meditation, and memory and we will outline how you can learn to meditate effectively and achieve a state of waking mindfulness throughout each day. You will also learn about the critical links between creativity and memory, and how to harness your creativity to improve your memory skills. Additionally, you will discover that you have the ability to transform your emotional habits to further improve your memory.

The last two chapters of this guide cover tips and techniques for learning information, whether it is small amounts or overwhelming lists of information. You will learn enough to train yourself to memorize with the best of them and reach the levels of competitive memorization if you wish. Believe it or not, with the techniques in this book you can learn to memorize a randomly shuffled full deck of cards or even a set of dominos in random order.

There are plenty of books on this subject on the market, so thanks again for choosing this one! Every effort was made to ensure it is full of as much useful information as possible. Please enjoy!

Chapter 1: What is Photographic Memory?

Photographic memory is the supposed ability to take a mental snapshot and be able to recall it in perfect detail in the future. Unfortunately for many readers, this book begins with a massive disappointment. Brace yourself...are you ready? Here it is: *photographic memory is a myth!*

Yes, we are telling you the truth. Although the idea of having a photographic memory is quite popular, often perpetuated by exaggerated stories of spies, famous leaders or ordinary people who could supposedly store mental snapshots and recall them later in perfect detail, there is no recorded proof of anyone with a memory like this. In each case of a person claiming to have a "photographic memory," there has always turned out to be some other explanation for the person's apparent perfect recall. There is one possible exception. In the 1970s, one woman demonstrated an impressive ability that is closer to photographic memory than any recorded ability before or since. The researcher tested her by first showing her a partial image while she had one eye closed. A couple of days later, she would look at the other part of that image with the other eye. She was able to retain the mental picture of the first image and combine the two partial images in her brain so that she could tell the researcher what the whole image looked like.

However, that woman's abilities were never fully tested or confirmed. She ended up marrying the researcher who studied her. After the marriage, she was never the subject of memory testing again. Not enough data on her abilities exists to conclusively prove her memory abilities, and no study participants were able to reproduce her supposed abilities when another researcher decided to investigate the claims made by this woman's researcher husband. As a result, the claim of having a "photographic memory" remains unreliable to this day.

Eidetic Memory

Photographic memory is sometimes confused with an eidetic memory, which is real but very rare. Eidetic memory is a phenomenon in which a vivid "afterimage" of something remains in the mind for up to a few minutes after the original image was seen. This phenomenon gives the person extremely accurate recall abilities, but this recall is never perfect. Eidetic memory exists in 2 to 15 percent of children and very few adults. There are existing claims that you can train yourself to have an eidetic memory, but these are false; an eidetic memory is a quality that you either have or do not have.

But There is Still Great News!

Now that you are feeling disappointed and discouraged about your non-existent potential to achieve photographic or eidetic memory, you are probably asking yourself why you bothered to look at this book. Do not fear, because there is still much that can be learned!

Now that we have disappointed you, the good news is that the term "photographic memory" is still immensely popular and a widely accepted term for having the ability to recall experiences with great detail and clarity. So as far as the general population is concerned, this book is about training your brain to have a photographic memory. If you read the instructions, follow the suggestions and practice the memory training techniques, you will be able to truthfully claim that you have a photographic memory, at least as far as the way that most people in society define that term. Only you (and a few others) know the truth!

Although you may not ever be able to recall an event or scene with such perfect clarity that you remember every single detail, you still have the potential to improve your memory to an astonishing degree! After practicing the methods in this book, many people have been able to quickly memorize the order of a randomly shuffled deck of cards or an entire set of dominoes placed in random order. Other than these party tricks, you can also train your brain to retain critical information, such as quickly recalling faces and names, remembering long lists of information without having it written down, or easily reciting the directions to a location after only hearing it one time. So, have hope – although you may never achieve the mythical "photographic memory," if you follow the instructions in this book for training your brain, you can make many people *think* you have a photographic memory!

How Does Memory Work?
Before we get into training your brain, let's take a look at how the memory process works so you have a clearer understanding of what you are trying to master.

When we talk about **memory**, we are talking about the process by which the brain acquires, stores, retains and later retrieves information. There are three major processes in memory: **encoding, storage,** and **retrieval**.

When we experience an event, person, place or thing, the details of that experience are translated through our perception, the involvement of our five senses in the experience. This is the beginning of the **encoding** process.

Details about sight, sounds, touch, smell, and taste are all transmitted to the hippocampus, which is a part of the brain that puts all of the details together into a single experience. Scientists believe that the hippocampus and another part of the brain called the frontal cortex to analyze experiences and "decide" if they're worth storing for long-term memory.

Once your senses have perceived an experience, chemical and electric messages fire between nerve cells, forming a specific pathway within the brain. This specific pathway is related to that experience, and the more times you encounter that experience, the stronger that pathway becomes.

An experience can only be properly encoded if you are paying attention; thankfully, the brain filters out most of what we encounter on a daily basis. Without this filter, our memories would be full within the first hour of a day!

After encoding comes the **storage** process of the memory. A sensation is first stored in **short-term memory**, which can typically only hold approximately 7 items at a time for about 30 seconds. If the information is important, it will be repeated and used often, which leads to it being stored in **long-term memory**. After the information has moved to this part of the memory, it is called "**retained**" memory. Your long-term memory has an amazing capacity. So far, there seems to be no limit to the amount of information it can store or the length of time that it can store it.

When we want to remember something, our brain goes through the **retrieval** process, which brings the information back from our unconscious mind to our conscious mind. When we have trouble remembering something, it is often because it was not properly encoded or stored in the first place. This happens often when we are distracted. This distraction could be due to stress, excessive strong emotions, or too much going on around you. Or if you are having trouble remembering something that you studied, it may be because you studied in an environment that was not conducive to studying or because you did not repeat the information to yourself often enough. In other words, you are responsible for making sure that important information is properly encoded and stored so that you can recall it when you need to.

Many people think of themselves as having "good" or "bad" memories, but the truth is that most people have the same potential for memory ability, assuming there are no underlying conditions damaging brain function. Since almost all of us have the potential to achieve phenomenal recall abilities, that means that the techniques in this book could turn you from someone who has a "bad" or average memory to someone who remembers great quantities of information with seemingly minimal effort!

Chapter 2: Eating for Better Memory

Since our nutrition – or lack thereof – has a huge impact on our physical and emotional fitness, it

only makes sense that healthy eating can be hugely beneficial to our ability to recall facts and experiences. This chapter will

cover the various nutrients that you should incorporate into your diet for better brain health and improved memory, as well as the foods that you should avoid if you're hoping to improve your recall skills.

1. **Omega-3's**: Lately it seems that you cannot get through a day without hearing another expert touting the benefits of omega-3's, and the memory experts are no exception! These oils are found in fatty fish, like salmon, halibut, and tuna, and they play an important role in brain function. A 2016 study released by Harvard Medical School shows that these powerful –

albeit smelly – oils can reverse the decline of memory, too. If you do not like eating the types of fish rich in this type of oil, consider taking a fish oil supplement that includes plenty of Omega-3's.

If you do invest in an Omega-3 supplement, just make sure that it is a supplement that has been verified by the United States Pharmacopeia, or USP. This verification means that it has been analyzed and tests have confirmed that it contains the ingredients that are printed on the label, and that the potency of the nutrients is accurate. It also means that there are no harmful substances that were accidentally included and that the desirable nutrients will absorb into your body when you take the supplement. Look for a little "USP Verified" mark on any supplements that you purchase!

2. **Fruits and Vegetables**: Omega-3 oils are known to reduce inflammation, but what about other anti-inflammatory foods? In general, foods that are high in antioxidants help lower inflammation in the body. You can find high levels of antioxidants in many fruits and vegetables. As it turns out, these foods have a significant impact on your mental health, too. People who eat a wide variety of vegetables and fruits are at decreased risks of developing dementia or any other age-related type of mental decline than people who eat less healthy foods. This has been proven by multiple studies over decades of research.

3. **Caffeine:** Coffee-lovers, rejoice! Recent research from the Radiological Society of North America has shown that drinking just 2 cups of coffee per day can help

boost short-term memory function. Additional research has also shown that *when* you consume caffeine makes a difference, too. One study shows that taking a supplement containing caffeine was beneficial to students' memories if they took it right after learning some new information. The benefits from the caffeine were shown to last for up to 24 hours.

4. **Vitamin D:** This nutrient is essential to many functions of the body, including memory. More than one study in recent years has linked low levels of vitamin D with quicker memory loss and greater risks of dementia than those who have healthy levels of vitamin D. Many people are at risk of being deficient of vitamin D, especially those of us who live in cold climates. Supplements for this vitamin are widely available, but you should ask your doctor to test your vitamin D levels before taking a supplement. Again, make sure to look for a "USP Verified" stamp of approval on your vitamin bottle.

5. **Cocoa:** Like fruits and vegetables, cocoa is rich in antioxidants. These particular antioxidants are called flavonoids, and they are quite helpful to the brain because they encourage brain cells and blood vessels in the brain to grow. They also cause more blood to flow to the brain segments that take part in memory encoding and storage. More blood flow means more oxygen and nutrients are going to these areas, so it is great for your memory! Flavonoids are most dense in dark chocolate and non-existent in white chocolate, so the most memory benefits can be derived from eating chocolate with 70% cacao or higher. Incidentally, the

consumption of dark chocolate has also been associated with a higher visual function. Eating just a little of high-quality dark chocolate each day has many proven benefits to your health, so this added bonus of improved memory should have us all jumping for a (small) chocolate bar!

6. **Protein:** Along with benefits to muscle and endurance, protein has also been proven to improve memory. One study showed that eating a protein-heavy breakfast enhanced the accuracy of short-term memory, possibly because eating more protein leads to more stable glucose levels in the blood. Consider adding some lean sources of protein to your breakfast, like eggs and turkey bacon, to improve your short-term memory abilities.

7. **Choline:** Here's another great reason to eat eggs! A nutrient called choline can instantly boost short-term memory, and just one little egg yolk contains 115 mg of choline. The benefit of this nutrient to short-term memory has been shown in several studies. There are many ways to incorporate eggs into your diet, so get creative and eat your eggs!

8. **Luteolin:** This nutrient, found in celery and peppers, fights the type of brain inflammation that can come with aging. With the reduction of brain inflammation comes a reduced risk of age-related memory problems. The takeaway is to eat sources of this nutrient if you want to stay sharp as you age! It is okay if you do not enjoy raw peppers or celery. These vegetables can be

cooked and added to a variety of delicious recipes, including soups, stews, and stir-fry dinners.

9. **Less Added Sugar and Refined Carbs:** Eating foods with a lot of added sugar, such as that found in sodas and candy, has been linked with poor short-term memory. Additionally, people who ate foods with high added sugar have reduced brain volumes and overall poorer memory abilities. If you do enjoy sweetened beverages and food, try plain beverages (like iced tea) or unsweetened cereal and just adding a little sugar or honey. This will cut your sugar intake immensely since pre-sweetened foods typically have much more sugar than you are likely to add on your own.

   Highly refined carbohydrates, like those found in cereals, white rice, cookies, and white bread can also be dangerous. These processed carbs cause the sugar levels in your blood to suddenly and rapidly increase as they are digested. Large fluctuations in blood sugar levels are dangerous for many parts of your body, and one result can be reduced functioning of the brain. On top of that, a study of children showed that those who ate more refined carbs had poorer short-term and working memories. The foods they ate included french fries and noodles. Instead of consuming these highly refined carbohydrates, try incorporating whole grains and complex carbs such as sweet potatoes into your diet.

10. **Less Alcohol:** Alcohol is worth cutting back on, too. While occasional controlled drinking is not harmful, researchers have found proof that binge drinking

(quickly consuming enough alcohol to raise the blood alcohol levels above the legal limit) causes difficulties in memory recall and can damage the hippocampus. If you will recall from Chapter 1, the hippocampus is important in the brain's memory storage process. If you find yourself at a party or other situation where you might normally binge drink, try limiting yourself to one drink per hour and drink a glass of water in between alcoholic beverages. If you find you are unable to stop or control your drinking, there are many options for getting help. Your future memory ability depends on it!

11. **Red Wine:** Although binge drinking is clearly unhealthy for many reasons, research has shown that a glass or two of red wine can be beneficial. Red wine contains a compound called *resveratrol*, which acts as an antioxidant and has many health benefits, including the slowing and possible reversal of age-related memory loss. If you're not into red wine, have no fear. The compound is also found in red grapes, some berries, and peanuts. There are also some supplements available, but ask a health expert before taking one.

If your head is spinning just a little from all this nutritional advice, here's a quick summary: Eat fish with Omega-3's or find a good supplement for this nutrient. Eat a lot of different fruits and vegetables and include a moderate amount of caffeine in your diet. Ask your doctor to test your vitamin D levels and take a supplement if needed. Eat a small amount of dark chocolate and drink one or two glasses of red wine every now and then. Eat plenty of lean protein, including eggs, and incorporate celery and peppers into your diet. Limit the number of sugary foods and drinks you consume, and avoid refined carbs. Try to avoid binge drinking altogether.

There are plenty of delicious ways to incorporate all these suggestions into your diet, so enjoy! Keep reading to find the next step to a superb memory.

Chapter 3: Exercise Your Way to Improved Recall

Now that you know how to eat for maximum recall ability, let's talk about exercise.

It is not everyone's favorite topic, but it is a necessity nonetheless. You have heard the myriad of benefits to exercising from your doctor, magazines, news shows, and well-intentioned family members. Well, as it turns out, an exceptional memory is one more potential benefit of working out.

How Exercise Helps Memory

There are a ton of in-depth scientific studies that prove the positive link between exercise and improved memory, but the bottom line is that exercise increases your rate of circulation. An increased rate of circulation means that more oxygen is going to your brain, so it can function more efficiently. Specifically, researchers have found that exercising 4 hours or less after learning something new can help you to retain that information much better than if you had been inactive for a long time after learning. The reason for this seems to be that exercise causes a better flow of blood, leading to increased activity in the hippocampus of the brain.

On top of this benefit, exercise has been shown by multiple studies to improve overall brain function, including memory. One particular study showed that not only does exercise help prevent age-related memory loss, but it can *improve* your ability to retain and recall information! The results of this study showed that aerobic exercise (e.g., walking or running) and anaerobic exercise (e.g., weight lifting) each affected different types of memory, but the important result was that they both improved memory abilities. For the best overall improvement to your memory, then, the recommendation is to try and incorporate both aerobic and resistant types of exercise into your routine.

The Dangers of Not Working Out

Just in case you are still sitting on the couch and thinking that perhaps you can do without this part of your memory upgrade, you should also know that staying *inactive* can be very harmful to your brain function. One study on rats showed that a sedentary lifestyle causes the neurons (nerve cells) in the brains to have extra branches. At first, this sounds like a good thing, but it turns out that the extra branches are related to regulation of involuntary functions of the body, like breathing. The extra branches cause the nervous system to be overstimulated. This overstimulation can cause problems like damage to the heart or lungs and a dangerous increase to your blood pressure. Since leading an inactive lifestyle can have such a detrimental effect on the shape of your brain's nerve cells, just think about what the dangers to the rest of your brain's functions, like memory, might be!

If you're a true-blue couch potato and you feel like you might be allergic to exercise, you can try adding just little bits of exercise at a time. Even a brisk twenty-minute walk has been proven to increase activity in the brain. Twenty minutes is just a minuscule portion of your day when you think about it, and the benefits will far outweigh the risk of missing your couch for that amount of time! Go ahead and give it a try – we sincerely doubt that you'll be sorry.

Chapter 4: Catch Some Zzzzzzz's!

While we're on the topic of better health habits, we should talk about the one that is seriously lacking for most adults lately: sleep. Although caffeine in moderate amounts can benefit your memory, it is no substitute for a great night of sleep.

Sleep and Memory Consolidation
When we sleep, our brain goes through much of the process of *memory consolidation*, which is when recently learned experiences are sorted and the important ones are changed into long-term memories. Various structural and chemical changes in the nervous system cause this conversion, and much of this depends on us getting enough sleep. Some memory consolidation can happen when we are awake, but the most important parts happen when we are asleep.

Even if you can't get a full night of sleep, your memory abilities can benefit from a short nap! One study had two groups of adults memorize illustrated cards. One group took a forty-minute nap after memorizing, and the other group stayed awake for forty minutes. Then both groups were tested on how much they remembered from what they had previously memorized. To the surprise of the researchers, the group that took a nap showed significantly better recall abilities.

A similar study was performed on two groups of children who were in the age group of 10 to 14. Some of the children were given memory training, then they were tested on the same day. They did not sleep between the training and testing. The rest of the children were given memory training in the evening, allowed to sleep for a full night, and then tested in the morning. The results were that the group that was allowed to sleep before testing performed significantly better.

What Happens When We Don't Get Enough Sleep?
Since sleep is critical to proper memory storage, it follows that sleep deprivation causes problems in our ability to form new memories. It only takes a single night of sleep deprivation to significantly reduce our ability to retain any new information! This discovery is somewhat concerning, considering how sleep-deprived most adults are these days.

Not only does sleep deprivation hinder your ability to commit new information to memory, but it also negatively impacts your *working memory,* which is the brain's system for temporarily holding information available for processing while you perform complex tasks. In other words, it's your ability to work with information as it is given to you. It can also be called your short-term memory. It is critical to your ability to reason, make decisions and behave rationally.

When you are sleep deprived, your brain's functions are noticeably sluggish and it goes into a kind of "conservation mode," shutting down some of the more basic functions. Your working memory then steps in to make up for some of these basic functions to help us perform complex tasks. However, this system of compensation is not perfect. Research has shown that in this state, people are much more easily distracted and more likely to overreact to emotional stimuli. As a result, the working memory is compromised and we are less able to act rationally.

How Do We Get More Sleep?
People are busier than ever lately, and it can be easy to sacrifice sleep to pack more activity and productivity in your

day. But by now you should be able to see how critical sleep is to your goals of achieving superb memory abilities. If you wish to one day wow your friends and family with your remarkable memory or be able to memorize great quantities of information for work or school, you must make sleep a priority!

Experts recommend that adults of all ages get seven to nine hours of sleep per night. For you to achieve this, we suggest following these helpful hints:

- *Make a schedule* for sleep. Schedule your lights-out and wake-up times, and stick to them just as rigidly as you would a business meeting. Even on the weekend, when it's tempting to stay up late and sleep in, you need to stay committed to the same bedtimes and wake-up times.

- *Turn off the TV, computer and all mobile devices* an hour before your lights-out time. We have all heard of the studies that show how disruptive those bright, shiny screens are for our sleep. If we are looking at them too close to bedtime, the quality of our sleep can be significantly decreased.

- *Unplug or cover anything in your bedroom with standby lights.* Those little round red, blue, or green lights can be equally disruptive to the quality of your sleep, even if they seem small and insignificant. You may fall asleep with them in the room just fine, but just the presence of those lights can interfere with your brain waves while you sleep, and as a result, you do not sleep as restfully or as deeply.

- *Avoid alcohol and coffee after dinner.* It may seem that alcohol helps you sleep, but in all actuality, it keeps you from reaching the deep sleep that your memory needs. Caffeine may keep you awake or cause poor sleep quality, too.

If you follow these tips and make a sincere effort make sleep a high priority, we are confident that you will be reaping the memory benefits in as little as a few days.

Chapter 5: Memorable Meditation

When you picture someone who meditates regularly, you may picture a serenely calm person who is rational, grounded and in touch with their feelings. Or, if you have a less favorable opinion of meditation, you may form an entirely different picture in your head. But what you may not picture is someone who has a remarkable memory. The mental benefits of meditation have been studied and widely publicized for decades now, but many people may not be aware that memory is among them.

What is Meditation?
Meditation by definition is simply the practice of using various techniques to train attention and awareness, thereby achieving an emotionally calm and mentally clear state of being. There are a large variety of techniques that fall under the umbrella of meditation, including visualization, chanting, breathing techniques, various physical poses, guided practices, and focusing on particular objects, both real and imagined.

People who meditate may do so because they want to reduce stress, feel less physical or emotional pain, increase their inner peace or improve their breath control. You may have heard of many of its many benefits, including anxiety reduction, improved emotional health, lowered blood pressure, enhanced self-awareness and improved concentration. Some people find that they are able to sleep better once they have practiced meditation for a while, and others use it as part of their addiction recovery program. Most people who practice meditation find that they have a better overall feeling of well-being and compassion towards themselves and others. What many people may not realize is that by practicing meditation, they improve their overall brain function, including their memory.

How Does Meditation Improve Memory?

Essentially, meditation is an exercise that slows down your mind's processing. By practicing meditation, you train your mind and give yourself more control of your thoughts. Ultimately, this control can also greatly improve your memory.

You may recall that *working memory* is essentially the short-term memory, where new information is held temporarily to help you perform complex tasks. After these tasks, information that is useful may be committed to long-term memory. We use our working memory multiple times per day, whether it is helping us get to a new address or retaining the names of new business associates in a meeting. As it turns out, the working memory can be strengthened by meditation.

During a meditation practice, we pay attention to our thoughts; specifically, we either try to focus on one thought, process or object, or we simply sit and observe our thoughts without trying to control or react to them. Either way, we are much more focused than normal.

Through modern technology that allows brain scans, researchers have been able to get a good look at what happens in the brain before and after meditation practices. These brain scans have shown that meditation causes our brains to stop processing information as actively as they normally would. This sounds like it might be a bad thing, but it means that there is significantly more focus in a brain that has been trained by meditation. More focus means less anxiety, less distraction, and a much better ability to commit information to memory!

Researchers believe that the reason for this increased focus from meditation is that people gain better control over their *alpha waves*, which form a kind of screen for everyday distractions. When you are better able to block out distractions, you can process more important information better, thus increasing your chances of recalling it later. This ability has been shown to improve in as few as eight weeks of regular meditation, even in people who had never attempted meditation before.

Not only does meditation improve your ability to focus, but it also has been proven to cause an increase in the amount of the gray matter (which contains neuron cells) in your brain. This gray matter generally decreases with age, leading to decreased brain function and memory abilities. But thanks to its positive effects on gray matter and alpha-wave control, meditation can benefit memory abilities for people from all generations, including the elderly. Research has shown astonishing possibilities for the benefits of meditation to memory, notably the ability to help prevent Alzheimer's disease and dementia.

How to Incorporate Meditation into Your Life
Now that you know how great meditation can be for your capacity to remember, you're probably wondering how to get started. If you are a beginner to meditation, it's best to start small and build from there. Follow these tips to begin your very own meditation practice:

1. **Find a regular time during the day** that is most conducive for you to meditate. This could be at the

beginning of the day, lunchtime, right after work, or right before bed. The key is to find a time when distractions are minimal and you are best able to focus your mind.

2. Schedule just **5 minutes each day** and build from there. **Set a timer** when you start, so you don't need to keep glancing at the clock during your practice. At first, 5 minutes may seem far too long, but eventually, you'll get used to it and at that point, you may want to try for 10 minutes each day. But don't rush your progress.

3. **Find a comfortable place to sit**. You can sit in a chair with your feet down on the floor. If you would prefer, you can sit on the floor instead. If you need it, feel free to use a pillow or cushion for support. If you would like to try lying down, go ahead and do so, but some people do not recommend this.

4. Eventually, you may want to **create a meditation space** in your home, but this is not necessary when you're first starting out. Keep this in mind for the future.

5. An easy beginning meditation practice is to **count your breath**. Try counting each inhales and exhales with the same number, like this (thinking, not speaking aloud): "One" (inhale), "One" (exhale), "Two" (inhale), "Two" (exhale), and so on. Once you hit Ten, start over. Or you can just think to yourself, "In, out, in, out..."

6. **When your mind wanders** (which is normal and ok!), notice your distraction and then start paying attention to your breath again. Start counting again from the beginning if you do not remember where you left off. **Do not be upset with yourself** because you

let your mind wander! But do pat yourself on the back for the times that you notice that your attention has strayed because taking that notice means that you are becoming more aware of your thoughts.

7. Try **noticing sensations in your body** while you breathe, once you get used to the counting. Where do you notice the inhalations? And the exhalations? Do you feel any tightness or discomfort anywhere? If so, try focusing your breath energy on those areas and notice how the tightness gradually loosens up.

8. **When distracting thoughts arise**, try to just notice them without engaging them. Don't dive into them and try to solve them. Just acknowledge them and move on.

9. **Do this every day** to make it a habit. After many weeks (possibly months, if you're a tough sell), it will become as habitual as making your bed or brushing your teeth.

10. **If you feel like nothing is changing** as a result of your meditation practice, be patient. Meditation is not about finding profound insights or suddenly becoming serene and wise. It is about accepting your thoughts and surroundings without judgment in each passing moment. You are probably changing gradually without even realizing it, gaining attributes like greater concentration, self-control, and the memory capacity that we are seeking.

If you are interested in delving further into meditation, enhancing your practice or just learning more, there are plenty of resources out there. YouTube offers many guided meditation channels, your Google Play or iTunes stores have meditation apps, the internet offers blogs and forums aplenty, and your local library has books and videos that can guide you. The important part is to keep learning and practicing. The ultimate goal of this book is to improve your memory ability, but you may reap a myriad of benefits by pursuing an interest in meditation!

Chapter 6: The Art and Science of Being Mindful

Right now, you may be thinking that there is no need to cover mindfulness. *"Didn't we just cover that in the meditation chapter??!"* Well, yes and no. While it is true that meditation helps you achieve a state of mindfulness, the two concepts are not necessarily intrinsically linked.

What is Mindfulness?
Mindfulness refers to the state of being aware of your thoughts, feelings, and surroundings at any given moment, whether or not you are meditating. "Being present" is a description often given to people when they are mindful. Meditation can be the formal practice of mindfulness, but mindfulness by itself is something that you can practice in any situation.

In general, people have a bad habit of focusing on the negative and overlooking the positive parts of life. We can be so ruled by regrets from the past or anxieties of the future that we are unaware of our present situation. We are also quick to label thoughts, feelings, and circumstances as "good" or "bad." In contrast, when we are mindful, we carefully observe our thoughts and feelings without labeling or judging them.

Mindfulness can be a healthy way to become aware of emotions that you hide under the surface. Without you being aware of them, these hidden emotions can be causing problems in relationships or distracting you from focusing on your current situation. Mindfulness means simply living in each moment instead of focusing on the past or present.

There are a great number of benefits to practicing mindfulness in your daily life, including improved relationships, decreased depression and anxiety, lowered stress levels and improved overall health. Additionally, mindfulness training can improve your concentration and memory.

Mindfulness and Memory
Similar to meditation practice, mindfulness training helps you filter out distracting and potentially damaging thoughts so that you can focus on information as it is given to you. This increased focus leads to better information storage and consequently better recall of what you have learned and experienced.

A 2016 study of almost 300 students in the field of psychology showed that mindfulness training can improve your ability to recall objects through your recognition-memory, which is what you use to recognize people or things that you have seen before. On top of this, mindfulness training has also been shown to reduce the risk of decline in brain function associated with aging.

How to Bring More Mindfulness to Each Day
A great beginning to mindfulness is the meditation practice we discussed in chapter 5. However, there are many more ways to begin practicing mindfulness in your daily life. Try each of the following suggestions and take note of which ones seem the most effective for you:
- **Mindful listening:** When listening to another person, many of us have the bad habit of letting our minds wander and not being fully present. We think about the other person, but not always what they are saying. Or we are completely distracted by our own thoughts or surroundings while only pretending to listen! The next

time you are listening to someone, whether they are someone you love or not, try using this time to exercise mindfulness. Focus all your attention on that person and what they are saying, even if it seems mundane and unimportant. They will truly appreciate the attention and may decide to reciprocate and give you more attention the next time you speak.

- **Household chores:** Since most of us spend a good deal of time doing household chores, these are excellent opportunities to practice mindfulness. The next time you have to fold laundry, wash dishes or make dinner, try focusing your entire attention to that particular task, and continue to focus on it as each moment. Notice the aromas of the food you cook and watch the transformation the raw ingredients go through as you combine and heat them to make a dish. Pay attention to the textures of the clothes you fold, the sounds that the dishes make as they bump into each other in the soapy water, and the light and temperature of the room you're in. As you practice this mindfulness, you'll begin to feel that each little act is a special ritual. You will be in tune with your world and able to transform ordinary chores into harmonious parts of your day.

- **Mindful Eating:** Since most of us have lives that are jam-packed with activities, we often eat meals on the run, while making phone calls or driving to the next practice or event. Fast food is a staple in our diet, and many families rarely sit down to eat dinner together – and when they do, it's often in front of the television. Try bringing mindfulness to one meal per day to start off. Sit down in a designated eating space with no distractions. Leave the cell phone in another room and turn off the TV. Take time to savor each bite, noticing the texture, flavor, and aroma of your food. Take small bites and eat slowly, and pay attention to how your body feels as you nourish it. Notice when you feel full and make a point of ending the meal right then. This practice is not only good for your brain, but it has the added benefit of aiding healthy digestion and weight loss. Soon you'll find that you want to practice mindfulness every time you eat, and those fast food meals will be a thing of the past!

- **No More Multi-tasking!** Lately, the ability to "multi-task" has been considered a virtue, something that we like to brag about when talking to friends, family or potential employers. But the truth is that multi-tasking is the opposite of productive; it spreads out attention too thin and makes us more liable to make mistakes. Instead of trying to do multiple things at a time, focus on one task at a time. Pay attention to phone conversations, answer emails while focusing solely on the computer screen and keep your attention on the present discussion in meetings instead of surreptitiously checking the messages on your phone. You will be amazed at how much more you are able to remember from each part of your day and the improved quality and efficiency of your work.

- **Stop Rushing:** All too often, we try to get things done as quickly as possible so that we can move on to the next thing. We focus on deadlines, productivity and the number of tasks that we can pack into a day instead of appreciating each moment as it comes. Try slowing your pace down physically for a change and see what happens. When you go grocery shopping, pay attention to each item as you check it off your list. Drive and walk at reasonable speeds instead of rushing to shave minutes off your commute. Take the time to connect with a client instead of being focused on a quick sale. You'll find that you take away value from each experience when the goal is to be present instead of moving as quickly as possible.

- **Mindful Movement:** Whether you are exercising or just walking between offices at work, pay attention to the sensations in your body. Appreciate the movements of each limb and the feelings of your feet as they hit the ground beneath you. Notice how your clothes feel as they move against your skin. Take note of all of the little characteristics of the scene around you, whether you are indoors or outdoors. This mindfulness is a practice you can incorporate into your day without taking any extra time in your busy schedule. You may find that you appreciate your body and ability to move much more if you are mindful of each individual movement.

- **Take some time to do "nothing.":** Our culture applauds productivity and frowns on idleness, so most of us have lost the ability to sit still and do nothing at all. In fact, we tend to feel guilty if we even consider spending time doing "nothing." But the fact of the matter is that we really do not need to be focused on a task at every moment of the day! Try taking a little bit of "nothing" time each day, even if you are only able to do so for just a few minutes. Set a timer if you need to, then sit silently in your favorite chair or couch. Sit outside in the sun if the weather is pleasant, or go to a favorite park and enjoy a gentle breeze. You might be surprised at how much pleasure you derive from just a few minutes of just "being" while doing nothing at all.

- **Notice Your Senses:** Another mindfulness practice is to notice your five senses in any given moment. Pay attention to smells as you go about your day. Listen to quiet noises outside your window or even in the same room: the hum of your computer, the washing machine in the other room, or the murmured voices of a quiet conversation down the hall. Notice the breeze on your skin, drops of rain on your face or the feel of a favorite shirt on your arms. Take a few moments to appreciate sights that you normally take for granted, like the sky during your evening commute, trees in the parking lot or children playing outside the school when you pick up your child in the afternoon. Notice the taste of your morning coffee as you sip it while catching up on email. Bringing awareness to your senses like this helps you to be engaged in each moment, instead of being preoccupied with distracting thoughts. You may even find that this sensory awareness brings a new sense of amazement to previous moments that seemed commonplace.

Following these suggestions for mindfulness training should help you to be more present in each moment as it passes. Not only will you reap the benefits of reduced stress, lowered anxiety and depression, and heightened sensory awareness, but you will notice that you remember so much more from each day. As you bring mindfulness into each day, your memory abilities will be strengthened because you are paying attention to so many more details that used to pass you by unnoticed.

Chapter 7: A Busy Mind Remembers More!

It seems counterintuitive that, after two chapters describing the benefits of slowing down, paying attention and making time to be still, we should follow with a chapter professing that you need to keep your mind busy! This is one of those cases in which it's best to strike a happy medium. If you want to improve your memory, it is critical to learn the meditation and mindfulness practices previously outlined. However, you do not want to give yourself *too much* downtime, because the memory functions of people who allow themselves too much idle time tend to suffer.

Keep Your Calendar Full
While it is important to allow yourself time to be mindful, exercise and get enough sleep, you should also make sure you are living a full and well-rounded life. Specifically, this means keeping busy with hobbies and a social life. Most people who are in school or work full-time while raising children do not have to worry about this problem. Usually, they have more than enough to do between school fundraisers, study groups, playdates, sports practices and family time. However, people who are not busy with family or a full-time career could benefit from this advice.

Many people over the age of 50, who are retired, single or empty-nesters may want to try making sure they keep enough to do on their calendar. One study surveyed 330 adults ages 50 to 89 on the busyness of their calendar. Participants were asked to rate their day-to-day busyness, and they answered various questions about their schedule so that researchers could gauge how active their lives were. The participants also underwent tests that measured their memory abilities along with information processing speed, vocabulary and reasoning abilities.

The results of this test were that, on average, the adults who kept a busier life had better cognitive function scores than those whose calendars were comparatively empty. One researcher noted that the study did not thoroughly address whether a busy life improved cognitive function or vice versa, but it was speculated that staying busy and active might stimulate the brain, leading to intellectual growth. Specifically, keeping busy gives you more opportunities to meet new people and encounter new situations, which accelerates your brain's learning and growth. Since memory is a huge part of the cognitive function, it should be no surprise that staying busy helps people's memory abilities as well. The study noted that the two types of memory that are benefited from a busy calendar are *working memory* (a.k.a. short-term memory, previously defined in Chapters 4 and 5) and *episodic memory* (memory involved in recalling times and places).

The Dangers of Idleness

Although retirement is something that most Americans take for granted as the inevitable reward for their decades of work, retirement is actually a very recent and – some might argue – unnatural development to our culture. For thousands of years, humans kept working until physically unable to do so, simply because they had to and because that was how things were done. It is only in the past one hundred years or so that many of us have been retiring from work once we reach a certain age. In the 1800s, most men over the age of sixty-five were still working, but now that age is often considered the "golden age" when we can retire to a life of blissful ease.

Unfortunately, it seems that retirement may put your mental skills at high risk of decline. A 2010 study of thousands of retirees in America and Europe discovered that retirement leads to a reduction of thinking along with the long-anticipated reduction of physical labor. If you have ever taken a long vacation from work or school, you have probably experienced this phenomenon to a certain extent. When you return from vacation, you often find that you have to put extra mental effort into tasks that came easily before you left. When you relax, you no longer have the pressure of having to think creatively, find solutions to problems, impress potential clients or meet deadlines. While relaxation itself is not intrinsically a bad thing, this is a case in which too much of a good thing can be damaging.

The study mentioned in the previous paragraph used a test that included remembering lists of words. The researchers administered this cognitive test to the thousands of retirees they studied, and to senior adults who were still working. When they compiled their data, they specifically compared the cognitive skills of workers in their fifties to those of retirees in their sixties. Their finding, among other data, was that the more likely the sixty-somethings were to be retired, the worse their cognitive skills were in comparison to the younger group! Another conclusion drawn from this multi-country study is that the later you retire, the smarter you typically remain. Although many of us in America envy those in certain European countries who are able to retire at younger ages, the reality is that we keep our minds and memories sharper in America by continuing to work later in life.

Another factor of retirement and/or growing older that leads to quieter lives is decreased social interaction. When people your age or older pass away or move to sunnier climes, you may find that you can go entire days without speaking to anyone other than your pet cat. Unfortunately, a shrinking social circle can be as damaging to your brain function as leaving the workforce. When you interact with other people, you are forced to expand your perspective and think creatively. By keeping other people's experiences and opinions in mind, you exercise your working memory. You also constantly learn from the stories and information that they share with you. It follows that the fewer relationships you have, the fewer opportunities you have to engage your working memory. Your world shrinks, and so does the amount of information that you need to recall on a regular basis.

What Does This Mean for You?
As much as you may hate the idea of working into your late sixties or even longer, your memory will remain much sharper if you do so. If physical disadvantages, financial independence or other circumstances lead you to early retirement, make goals to keep yourself busy and social.

However, please do keep in mind everything that you have already learned in the previous chapters of this book. If you keep *too* busy, you most likely don't make time to eat properly, the quality and quantity of your sleep suffer, you probably don't have time to exercise and you certainly aren't making time to meditate or practice mindfulness. Additionally, the stress hormones from being too busy might actually hurt the brain. With all these downsides, being over-busy is definitely not the key to improving your memory abilities!

Instead of staying busy simply for the sake of being busy, find things that are interesting and meaningful to you and fill your calendar with these things. Make social appointments with friends, try new hobbies that seem interesting and pay attention to community events. You can attend local lectures and performances, look into making day trips to nearby destinations, and volunteer for a worthy cause. You can also try getting involved in your church or some other social organization so that you continue to meet new people and form new relationships. There are many engaging activities that can fill your calendar without adding to your stress levels. Believe us, your brain will thank you!

The memory is basically like a muscle. When it is exercised, it stays in shape and even improves. However, if it is not used, it gets weaker and weaker. By staying in touch with other people and being involved in a variety of activities, you give your memory plenty of new information to chew on every single day. So keep "flexing" those memory muscles and keep your calendar full.

Chapter 8: Time for Some Creative Thinking

Whether you think of yourself as a creative person or not, within you lies a spark of creativity. Creativity is simply the use of imagination or original ideas, and we all have the potential to be creative. Even if you've never penned a story or poem, picked up a paintbrush or captured a beautiful picture through a camera lens, you can be a creative individual. Every person on earth has a unique perspective, a different view that frames the world, and this perspective is the frame by which memories are formed.

The Link Between Creativity and Memory
Since your memories are how you store, connect or interpret your experiences, your memories actually reflect your individual creativity. You may remember a certain person that you saw last week because they looked a little like your Aunt Sally, or that bakery across the street might spark memories of your mother's apple pie. A beautiful painting in a shop window might bring back memories of a rainbow you saw as a child. Whatever your memories and intellectual connections might be, they are unique to *you* alone, and they show your potential to be creative.

Not only are memory and creativity intrinsically linked, but you can also boost your memory powers by exercising your creativity. When you strive to be creative, either by coming up with new ideas or making something artistically fresh, you draw on your prior experiences, whether or not you are aware of it.

Many people think that creativity is the exact opposite of memory. After all, the things we remember already exist, while creativity strives to come up with something new and fresh, right? This seems true, but it is not exactly accurate. In truth, creative insights always come from combinations of material that already exists in our minds. There are no new ideas that simply appear out of thin air; you build on existing ideas to come up with new ones.

Your memories are the raw materials for your creativity. As a result, when you exercise your creative abilities, you force your brain to form new pathways between memories. As you become more creative and come up with seemingly "new" concepts, old experiences that once seemed like separate events can become linked in your mind. This process leads to stronger memories as you draw on them again and again.

Some of you may think that you are just "not creative." There is a widespread false conception that creativity is primarily found in the sensory arts. While it is true that creativity is most obvious in painting, dance, music, sculpting, etc., you can find the ability to be creative even in the most logical of activities. Scientists and mathematicians must be creative on a daily basis to come up with new links between data or new formulas to explain old phenomena. Even the most mundane activities can require creativity at times. You think creatively when you face daily problems that require quick solutions, like when you have to housetrain a puppy or clean up the mess from a broken dishwasher.

How to Boost Your Creativity
Since your memory abilities can be improved by exercising your powers of creativity, how exactly

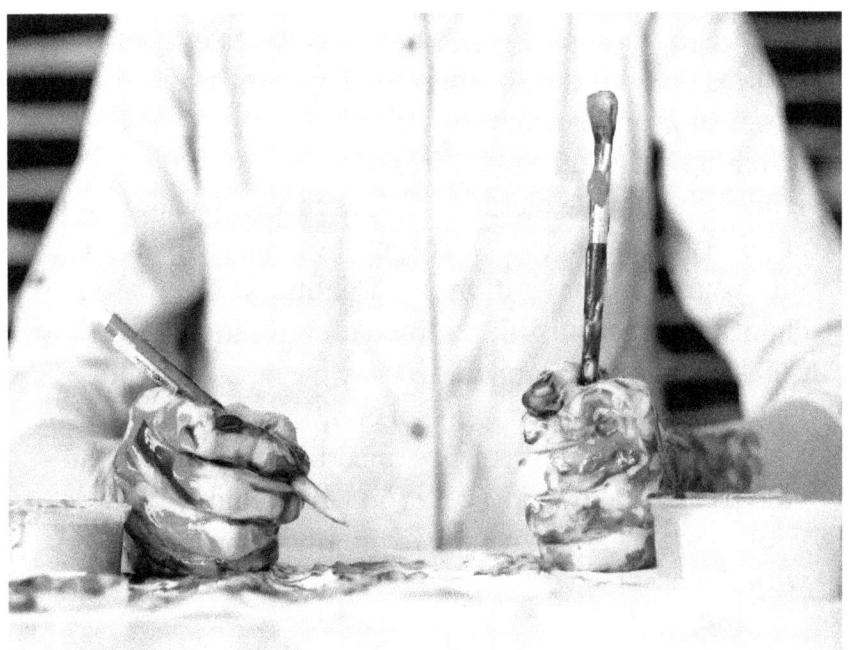

should you go about this process? Lucky for you, we've compiled a list of suggestions for flexing your creative muscles:

- **Cultivate boredom:** We spend so much time focused on finding entertainment that we rarely give our minds the opportunity to wander creatively. When we have downtime, we are quick to reach for the remote control or scroll through our phones in search of something to do. But if you make a point of reducing your entertainment, you give your creativity the opportunity to roam freely. Being "bored" prompts your brain to create something new, whether it is just wandering through ideas or coming up with something to do. To give this a try, go for a week without turning on your TV and see what kinds of ideas you come up with for entertaining yourself.

- **Daily creativity:** Schedule a time each day, even if just for 10 minutes, to do something creative. There are endless possibilities for this creative time! You can dance to your favorite tunes (don't worry, no one is watching), pick up a paintbrush for the first time since grade school, take pictures of flowers, or try your hand at poetry. You can even incorporate a creativity mantra into your daily meditation (see Chapter 5). Try chanting something like "I live a creative life" as you sit quietly and breath, and allow creative ideas to flood your mind. Repeat this time of creativity daily for at least 3 weeks, even if you are uncertain or feeling a tad embarrassed about doing it. You will probably find that your thoughts about your own creativity will change with the passing weeks.

- **Observe creativity:** Gather inspiration from the creativity of others. Go to art museums, listen to music and attend dance performances. You can even get inspired by the creativity of nature by going for a walk in the woods. Bring your binoculars!

- **Do everyday things in a different way:** When you take your everyday tasks and force yourself to do them differently, you make your brain think more creatively. For a change, try writing with your non-dominant hand or driving to work via a completely new and different route. Exercise in the morning if you usually go to the gym at night or vice versa. Eat breakfast for dinner. Hand-write a letter instead of typing an email. Visit a new place on the weekend, or eat a fruit that you have never tried.

- **Make a creative space:** If you have a whole extra room in your house, use this; otherwise, a corner of a room will work just fine. Set aside this space for any creative endeavors that interest you. Bring in any tools that you might use for your creating, display anything you have already made, and put up inspiration from other creators that you admire. Try putting up little notes to yourself that remind you that you are creative and you are an artist! It may feel cheesy, but it really works.

- **Give yourself time:** Creativity cannot be forced. If you find that, in spite of your best efforts, the creative juices aren't flowing, just relax and notice your thoughts and feelings. You may find that inspiration hits you at the strangest of times.

- **Rewire your inner critic:** Criticizing your own efforts may have its time and place eventually, but the inner critic has no place in your early efforts. Do not let anxiety or negative self-talk keep you from trying! Remind yourself that all creative artists started from somewhere, and you have the same potential as any of them. It is ok to acknowledge your anxiety and the reasons behind it, but talk back to it and then let it go. Allow yourself to make mistakes, because these are part of the creative process. If you find that inner criticism is still blocking you, incorporate positive affirmations into your meditations (again, see Chapter 5). An example is "I am fine just as I am." When you breathe in, think "I am fine..."; when you breathe out, think "just as I am..." Make your inhales and exhales long, slow and deep, lasting for 5 seconds each if possible.

- **Get moving**: People tend to have more creative ideas after exercise. Physical activity clears the mind, improves mood and raises energy for a significant period of time afterward. Just 20 minutes of aerobic exercise can help free your creative ideas. You may want to bring along a pencil and a little bit of paper, though – you never know when a creative idea may strike you!

- **Stretch your muscles:** After your period of aerobic exercise, be sure to stretch out your muscles. This helps to bring oxygen to your brain and symbolically releases any emotional blocks. Try standing tall and extending your arms behind you. Then stretch your arms to the sides and gently twist your spine to one side, then the other. Gently stretch your neck by lowering your head to one shoulder, then the other. Bend at the waist and reach towards your toes.

- **Bring your creativity with you:** Carry a notebook and pen with you or a handheld recorder. You never know when inspiration may strike you, and you want to be able to record it when it does!

- **Practice mindfulness:** See Chapter 6 for a full description!

- **Ask questions:** You can spark your creative thinking by wondering about things that have previously escaped your attention. How does a water filter work? How many hairs are on your head? At what rate do your fingernails grow? How many gallons of water are in the nearest lake? By questioning things that you don't normally think about, you create new pathways in your brain and open up potential new lines of investigation to pursue.

- **Say "Yes!":** When someone invites you to see an eclectic music group or try a new restaurant, say yes! When someone suggests a group camping trip or taking a dance class, give it a try. It probably won't hurt you…and you will likely come home with some new ideas, or at least an entertaining story or two.

- **Find a creative community:** Many productive artists find inspiration from each other. Find a group with similar interests to your own, such as a knitting group, painting class, choir, writing group, or improv troupe. If you cannot find a group, make one! Try posting invitations at local coffee shops or searching online forums for people with similar creative interests.

- **Imitate:** You've heard that imitation is the most sincere form of flattery. This is true, but it can also be a source of inspiration. Try recreating a favorite artist's work, but not exactly in the same way that they did it. For example, make it smaller or bigger, or transfer it to a different medium. If you love a particular painting, try recreating it with charcoal or colored pencils.

Imitate a favorite author's writing style, but use your own words.

Even if some of these suggestions seem a bit far-fetched or out of your comfort zone, that is sort of the whole point. Creative thinking stretches your imagination beyond your norm, whatever that may be. So, go ahead and give them all a try, at least once. You may be surprised at the results. Not only will you find yourself thinking more creatively than you thought possible, but your memory will begin functioning more efficiently with each creative endeavor.

The Reverse Holds True, Too
As it turns out, creativity and memory are so intrinsically linked that the relationship works in reverse. You have just learned how to think creatively in order to inspire your memory. But you will also find that your creative juices start to flow more freely as your memory abilities get sharper and stronger, too.

There is a reason that major creative breakthroughs tend to happen after a person has spent many years in their field. It is because they draw on previous experiences to come up with new ideas. It can take years, or even decades, to absorb the many small pieces of mental material that combine to feed a new insight. Old experiences are the raw material for creativity. As you strengthen your ability to recall memories, you may find that you are more creative than you ever imagined. This reciprocal relationship is both fascinating and exciting. Just imagine the creative possibilities that may open up for you as you flex your memory muscles!

Chapter 9: The Power of Emotional Recall

Of all the processes that go on in our brains, emotions are perhaps the most mysterious. It seems that these things that we call feelings are everywhere, inescapable, and sometimes so powerful that they temporarily incapacitate us. They are both visible and invisible, and they have connections to physical and spiritual sensations. They are the inspiration to many creative endeavors and the downfall of many otherwise powerful individuals. They have the power to ruin an entire week or create the greatest day of your life. But what are they?

What are Emotions?
By simplistic definition, emotions are natural states of mind caused by our circumstances, relationships or mood. But they are so much more than this. They are sensations generated by our brains that can affect our whole being, both physically and spiritually. They are combinations of physical stimuli, thoughts and the urge to act.

When we feel a powerful emotion, our body reacts with physical sensations. Your stomach can feel "jittery" when you are afraid. Your pulse quickens and you sweat when you are nervous or excited.

Emotions are also tied to thoughts. Although sometimes it's difficult to tell which came first, usually a specific thought leads to a specific emotion, although this succession usually happens so rapidly that you cannot separate the two without effort. Once you feel a specific emotion, you usually act on it in some small or large way. When you feel happy, you smile.

When you are sad, you may cry or lower your head. When you are angry, you may yell or even fight.

Emotions cause us to act in specific ways and say specific things, often without even meaning to. How many times have you said or done something in the heat of the moment, and then later regretted your emotional course of action? But the way you were feeling at the time was so powerful that you felt you had no choice but to act as you did.

Emotions and Memory
Since emotions are so closely tied to our words, actions and physical sensations, it makes sense that they have a very close relationship with memories. In fact, we are typically much more likely to remember a specific person, place, thing or event if it is tied with a powerful emotion or two. For example, you may have very little recollection of your math teacher in ninth grade because nothing particularly exciting ever happened in that class. However, during that same year, you may have had a History teacher who was always full of jokes and fascinating stories. He made you laugh and inspired you by his manner of teaching. Your feelings of humor, delight, and hope from your experiences with that particular teacher make him stand out in your memories.

In fact, recent research suggests that emotions, not personal significance, make certain experiences stand out in our memories. Sometimes emotions even warp our memories and make them inaccurate. If you are given instructions for a task, but then something happens that causes strong emotions, you may not be able to recall the instructions.

We also tend to treat memories differently depending on the emotions associated with them. If a memory is associated with unpleasant emotions, we might go to great lengths to avoid that memory. We may even go so far as to unconsciously block those memories, potentially to the point that we don't remember them at all. Sometimes extremely unpleasant memories, both conscious and unconscious, can be the root of serious psychological issues.

On the other hand, we like to retell the story of particularly happy or triumphant memories so that we can relive those more desirable emotions. We might remember the "happiest day of our life" in great detail, even down to exactly what we were wearing on that day.

Our emotions also affect our ability to recall past events. For example, when you are depressed, you are more likely to remember negative experiences. When you are experiencing an emotional "high," you recall other times when you have felt the same elevated mood. In other words, your mood when you *retrieve* a memory often matches the mood you were in when that memory was first *encoded* (see Chapter 1 for more about encoding and retrieval).

Using Emotions to Improve Memory Ability
When you simply allow emotions to affect physical reaction and your ability to recall experiences, you are ruled by your emotions. You give your feelings the power to keep you from remembering certain things and block important details. But by learning to *transform your emotional habits*, you can improve your overall recall ability for both past and future experiences. The idea is to be in touch with your emotions and accept them without letting them master you.

By practicing acceptance of your whole range of emotions, you will still be able to feel them but they will not be able to cloud your recall ability. An additional side benefit is that you will become less reactive to your emotions. You will have the power of choice over how you behave in situations, rather than your emotions telling you how to act and react.

Over the next several weeks, try each of the following suggestions to gradually transform your emotional habits and learn acceptance of your feelings:

- **Identify emotional triggers:** When you know that certain circumstances can cause specific emotions in you, you can be prepared for these feelings in advance even if you have no control over the triggers. In other words, forewarned is forearmed. Physical triggers can include other people's expressions or body postures, certain foods or beverages, medications, hormonal fluctuations, and illness. Mental triggers are things like religious beliefs of yourself and others, attitudes, comparisons to others, and making decisions. Environmental triggers can be certain types of weather, being in crowded places, or being isolated.

    Take some time to identify your emotional triggers. If there are any you can eliminate (like certain foods), get rid of them! Unfortunately, there is no way to get rid of the majority of our emotional triggers. But if you know in advance that you get anxious in crowds or nervous when you have to make a decision, you can prepare yourself for this in advance. Once you know what to expect, your emotions may not seem so bad. You'll find that you are able to experience them and know that they will come to an end once the trigger has passed.

- **Notice your inner talk:** The way that you speak to yourself can have a great impact on your emotions. When you are feeling worthless and depressed, it may be because you are telling yourself that you are worthless. Take a moment to ask yourself why you are feeling a certain way and what you have been telling yourself to fuel that emotion. Try reframing your inner talk in a more gentle and positive manner. Talk to yourself as you would a dear friend or a beloved child. Chances are that you are much harsher with yourself than you would be with anyone else, and you don't deserve that negativity! This change of inner talk can take a lot of practice, but do not give up.

- **Reframe problems**: Often, our emotions are caused by our perspective of a particular problem. For example, you may feel down because you made a mistake or you are experiencing a conflict with someone. Instead of being afraid, sad or anxious about this problem, try viewing it as an opportunity for growth and learning. Like changing your negative inner talk, this can take a lot of practice, because you are working to change years of a specific way of thinking and feeling. Be persistent, and you'll find that you become more optimistic about problems than you ever thought possible!

- **Sit with your emotions:** This is a particular form of mindfulness (further discussed in Chapter 6) that can be tremendously beneficial to transforming your emotional habits. When you are feeling a certain way (especially when you want to act on a strong emotion), take a moment to name it, either out loud or in your head. Then pause and focus on your breath as it goes in and out of your body, instead of acting. Next, get in touch with your physical sensations. Start by noticing your feet on the ground, or your seat and back on a chair. Then become aware of your heartbeat and any sensations in your stomach, chest, and throat. Keep breathing slowly in and out. Notice where you feel the emotion most strongly in your body and how it feels. Perhaps it is a prickly sensation in the back of your neck or a tightness in your chest. Maybe you associate certain sounds or smells with it.

As you explore the sensations with your emotion, resist the urge to act on them. Visualize moving the emotion into the area around your heart and pay attention to how it shifts. It may feel sharper at first, and then soften. Notice your perspective shifting.

Keep practicing this emotional awareness each time a strong emotion overtakes you. In time, you will find a new understanding of your emotions and the ability to regulate your response to them.

- **Express your emotions:** Although the idea is to not react to emotions, it is essential to still express them. Stifling strong feelings is dangerous to your physical and psychological well-being, so you must find appropriate ways to let them out. When you are angry, a brisk walk may help or you may need to scream into a pillow, or even pound on the pillow. When you are sad, you may benefit from a cleansing cry alone or on a friend's shoulder. If you find that you regularly experience anger or frustration, perhaps you should try enrolling in an exercise class or sports team. Physical activity is a great way of channeling strong emotions in an appropriate way. If you are grieving, journal about it, seek solace from a pet or a friend and give yourself time to work through the grief. One exception to emotional expression can be fear, so keep reading to learn how to handle feelings of fear.

- **Learn to tone down fear:** Repeated expressions of fear or reactions to things that strike fear in your heart can lead to phobias or panic attacks. Fear can take on a life of its own and gain the power to control all aspects of your life. When you are feeling fearful (unless you are actually in a dangerous situation; then, by all means, get away from it!), pause to notice the facts of the situation. What is happening in this exact moment? Notice your self-talk and tone down the fear from a catastrophic level to an approachable problem. Instead of picturing the worst possible outcome, picture yourself solving the problem and conquering your fear. Remind yourself that you have only been imagining one possible future, not the only one. Then imagine a new, more positive outcome.

- **Let emotional intensity fade:** When you are feeling strong emotions, take a timeout before acting. This "time out" could be any duration from a few minutes to a few days, depending on the situation. Give yourself appropriate healthy distractions, like exercise or creative outlets (see Chapter 8). Then revisit the problem or situation that is causing your emotions and see how you feel about it.

- **Try on opposite emotions**: If you are feeling a certain way that makes you uncomfortable, try challenging yourself to feel differently. If you are angry at someone, work to find things about them that you are grateful for. If you are envious of someone else's success, try being happy for them and celebrating their good fortune. These efforts will help you balance your emotions and ward off the tendency for resentment.

- **Laugh:** During particularly tense, frustrating or upsetting times, take a break to find some comedy. Look up stupid jokes or comedy sketches online. Even fake laughter has been known to help change your mood.

Emotions can be great teachers, once we learn to accept and even embrace them. Awareness of your emotions can teach you valuable lessons about yourself, like how you make choices, who your best friends are, and what your priorities are. Once you have learned to recognize and accept your emotions, you'll find that, with practice, you will have better ability to recall things that happen, no matter how you were feeling at the time.

Chapter 10: Small Tips and Tricks for Training Your Memory

So far, we have covered all of the health when it comes to better memory. We have covered your physical health, including diet, exercise, and sleep. We have also covered your psychological and spiritual health by teaching you how to meditate, be mindful, train your creativity and practice awareness and acceptance of your emotions. Each of these processes is a piece of the puzzle that lead to better brain health and stronger memory abilities. But we still have a few tricks up our sleeves.

You may be looking for helpful hints for studying for your next test or memorizing a speech for the next corporate banquet. Or perhaps you have started incorporating all of the healthy suggestions in the previous chapter and you are ready to impress your friends by becoming a true memory master. You will find the tips and techniques that you desire in these final two chapters. This chapter outlines easy ways to quickly memorize information, and the next chapter covers some major techniques for overhauling your memory powers.

No matter what you are trying to learn and remember, there are quite a few tricks that the memory experts swear by for better recall. Try the following ideas as you learn the key points of a presentation or study for an exam:

- **Take in information slowly**: It is pretty tempting to procrastinate on your studies and then "cram" for an exam, or to read as much of your textbook as possible so you can relax for the rest of the week. But you will find that memorization is more effective if you slow the pace of learning and take in the information over several days or even weeks. If you have an exam on ten chapters in a week, try studying two chapters per night, and then reviewing for a couple of days. If you are a teacher who needs to memorize the names of your students, learn four or five names per day and you should have the whole class memorized in a week or two.

- **Repetition is key**: You can hardly expect to memorize a large chunk of material in a few days, and then recall it again in a month without reviewing it in between. For long-term recall, you must repeat! Remember, new information represents a new pathway in your brain. If you want to remember the information and commit it to your long-term memory, you have to travel that pathway frequently! The more you review, the stronger the neural pathway gets. For example, if you are learning how to conjugate German verbs, set aside time to practice and recite the conjugations at least every other day for a couple weeks, then once every few days, then once a week.

- **Mnemonic devices:** A mnemonic device is any learning technique that helps you remember information. A classic example of this is the phrase "My Very Excellent Mother Just Served Us Nine Pizzas" for remembering the order of the nine planets. Or there is the rhyme for the months that helps you remember which of them have 31 days and which have 30 days. Or perhaps you have learned the method of keeping track of the month lengths by counting them on your knuckles. When it comes to these little memory tricks, the possibilities are endless as long as it helps you. If it is a list of things in a specific order, try coming up with a clever phrase, like the planet illustration. Or come up with a rhyme, song or image to help you remember.

- **Picture associations (visualization)**: A picture association or visualization is an image that you conjure in your brain by converting words to the nearest sounding word or words that you can think of. These are especially helpful when it comes to efforts to remember people's names. Someone named Shelly Baker could be visualized as wearing a baker's hat and apron, with pictures of shells on the apron. For someone named Ben, you can picture Big Ben in London, with Ben's face in place of the clock. For someone named Vincent, picture the famous self-portrait of the painter, van Gogh, only with Vincent's face in place of the painter's face. For someone named Sandy, imagine that person on a beach. The picture does not have to be anything special, just something that helps you remember.

- **Chewing gum:** It sounds a little silly, you may experience improved memory abilities if you try chewing some gum while you are learning some new information. This may not work, because only limited research has been done on the concept, but it is worth a try. One study suggested that participants had more accurate memory recall and better reaction times if they chewed gum. It has been speculated that chewing gum may increase activity in the hippocampus, which is involved in memory encoding and retrieval. Even if it may not work, it is certainly worth a try!

- **Mind mapping:** Mind mapping is a different way of visualizing information to make memorization easier. In this technique, you visually organize information in a way that makes it simpler to break into categories and remember systematically. The basic idea is to draw a diagram that shows relationships and the hierarchal organization of pieces of a whole. You draw a diagram, with the main idea at the center, and branches leading to sub-topics all around the main idea. The sub-topics can have more branches, or lists of simple details, drawn around them. An easy way to get good examples of this is to Google "mind map." You may find that you memorize information better by incorporating different colors into your mind map or writing in small and large letters to emphasize the importance of ideas.

- **"Chunking" information:** This idea correlates with taking in information slowly. Not only should you slow the rate at which you consume new material, but it helps to break it up into smaller, "bite-sized" pieces. If you are want to memorize an extremely long number, like the first 100 digits of pi, try breaking it into sequences of 10 numbers and memorizing the short sequences once at a time, like individual phone numbers. Other situations in which this technique might be helpful are memorizing speeches for weddings or monologues for a play.

All of the above techniques make use of the way that your memory already works, which is by associating old information with new information. In other words, when you take the familiar link it to something unfamiliar, the new and unfamiliar can become unforgettable. Each of them is tried and true, and the best part is that none of them require much time to help you. But if you're looking to memorize even more information, or continue to enhance your memory abilities to astonishing levels, read on to the next chapter.

Chapter 11: Becoming a Memory Champion

If you're not satisfied with boosting your brain health and learning various tips and tricks for various overall learning, this is the chapter you have been waiting for. This final chapter includes the techniques that those with the so-called "photographic memories" used to obtain memory greatness. These techniques are used by people who win memory championships and by those are employed by the military as spies. These are the people whose lives, or at least reputations, depend on having a superb memory. By using these techniques, you can reach the level of memory greatness that you have dreamed about!

The Military Method
Disclaimer: Although this method is touted as the "military method," there is no actual proof that this method is used by the military to train their operatives. However, it is suggested as a way of enhancing your ability to quickly memorize large amounts of information, and it has been touted by many as an effective method of training your memory. It does not take much time out of each day, so it is certainly worth a try!

The materials you will need for this method of memory training are a small bright lamp and a piece of darkly colored paper. You also need the written or typed book or document that you are planning to memorize.

Follow these steps:

1. Commit to approximately 15 minutes per day to practice.

2. Designate a quiet place in your house where you can practice. It is important that you are able to make the room dark, so use a closet if necessary. Bring your desk lamp in that area.

3. In your dark colored piece of paper, cut out a rectangle-shaped hole that is about the size of a paragraph on your document or book.

4. Put the paper on top of your document or book. Make sure that the paragraph you want to memorize first shows through the hole that you cut in the paper.

5. Place your document or book just far enough from your eyes to be able to see it easily and quickly.

6. Turn all of the lights off, and make sure the room is completely dark. Allow your eyes time to adjust to the darkness, so that you can begin to make out shapes in the darkness.

7. While looking at the place where your book or document is, turn on the small light for less than a second and then turn it off.

8. During that brief moment, your eyes will have taken a mental picture of the paragraph that shows through the

hole in your dark piece of paper. Focus on that image in your brain. When it has faded from your mind's eye completely, turn the lamp back on for another fraction of a second and then it off again. Always keep looking at the paragraph you are trying to memorize.

9. Do this repeatedly, for about 15 minutes every day, until you have the entire paragraph memorized without any errors whatsoever. Do not skip any days; according to some sources, skipping a day can set you back by an entire week.

10. If you use this technique, combined with all that you have already learned in this guide and the rest of the techniques described in this chapter, you will find that your memory is as close to "photographic" as you could ever imagine.

The Memory Palace
This method is a very powerful memory technique that has been proven to be effective, easy to learn, and a little fun to boot. It employs the method of visualization that you learned in the last chapter, but on a more complex level. Simply follow these steps to use this technique, and you will find it can be helpful in many situations:
1. **Choose a palace**. Although it is called a palace, it does not have to be a literal palace. Simply visualize a place with which you are extremely familiar. This can be your own home or school, for example. The key is to pick a place that you can easily picture in great detail. Also, try to visualize a specific walking route within your palace instead of just seeing it as a scene. So, if

your palace is your home, picture a specific order of walking through it, room by room. Other places that you could choose might be the place where you work, a local park or pathway that you walk or jog regularly, or familiar streets in your neighborhood.

2. **List Memorable and Important Features:** As you mentally tour your chosen palace, pay attention to the distinctive features in it. For example, if you chose your place of employ, the first feature might be the parking lot. Now walk your chosen pathway through your palace, taking note of each room or destination in the order that you have chosen. The more detail you notice, the better. Perhaps you scan each room from right to left, noticing features in order as you scan. Keep making mental notes of each feature as you go. Each feature that you notice will be a memory "slot" that you use later as you memorize pieces of information.

3. **Fully Imprint Your Palace in Your Mind:** Go through your memory palace over and over, making note of the same features each time until you have it fully memorized. This is important! If you do not have it completely and reliably memorized, the technique will not work for you. If necessary, write down each detail of your palace or draw a picture of it. Repeat your route through your palace aloud if that helps. Remember to always look at your chosen features of the palace in the same order and from the same perspective. Even when you think you have it fully memorized, go over it a few more times. You need to be confident in your knowledge of the palace and it is impossible to "overlearn" your mental path through it.

4. **Start using your palace:** Try using your palace to memorize something simple at first, like a grocery list. Start by visualizing the first thing on the list in association with the first feature of your palace. If the first feature of your palace is the parking lot and the first thing on your grocery list is eggs, picture eggs all over the parking lot. Picture little egg cars parked in the parking spots, smashed eggs all over the blacktop, and adorable winged eggs chirping happily in the trees. Got it? Next, let's say that the second feature of your memory palace is the front door of your office building and the second item on your grocery list is a carton of milk. Try picturing the front door as a milk carton, with lots of cold milk running out from under the door, forming little pools of milk around the entrance.

    Continue this visualization until you have placed each item on your grocery list firmly in association with a feature of your memory palace.

5. **Re-visit your palace:** Now that you have finished placing all of the items on your list, do some rehearsal. Repeat the journey once or twice so that you are sure you know the order of your list and you have not left anything out. If you have been successful at always starting at the same point and following the same route, your memorized list will come to your mind quickly as you visualize the pathway through your palace.

6. **Keep using your palace** to memorize longer lists and more intricate sets of information. You'll be

amazed at how much you can remember with this technique!

Peg System

This is another, somewhat simpler method of memorizing lists of information. It is simpler than the memory palace, but you may not be able to remember as much information with this one. The way it works is by pre-memorizing a simple list of words that are associated with numbers. The words that you memorize are the "pegs" in the system. It is generally useful to make the words rhyme with the numbers, or associate them with a well-known list, like the names of the seven books of the Harry Potter series.

For example:
One = sun
Two = glue
Three = key
Four = store
Five = drive
Six = bricks
Seven = Kevin
Eight = crate
Nine = line
Ten = pen

Next, when you need to remember a list of items, try associating each item from your list to the corresponding number peg. For example, we'll try another shopping list. If the first item on the list is bacon, picture a sun with bacon sizzling on its surface. If the second item is bread, picture a loaf of bread with all of the pieces stuck together with glue. Get the idea? If your list is longer than your peg system, you can repeat it in groupings of ten (or seven, if you are using

Harry Potter books). This method is simple but generally very

effective. If you are memorizing vast quantities of information, we suggest returning to the memory palace described above.

The Deck of Cards Memorization Method
Believe it or not, there are memory masters who can easily memorize the order of a randomly shuffled deck of 52 cards in less than two minutes! This feat is required in order to become a Grand Master of Memory at an official World Memory Championship (this is a real event).

One of these impressive card deck memorizers is Nelson Dellis, a four-time winner of the USA Memory Championship. When asked for a technique on how to memorize a shuffled deck of cards, he outlined the following steps:
   1. **Start with face cards.** Separate the face cards from the deck. There should be twelve of them: Jack, Queen, and King from all four suits. You'll start by just memorizing the order of these twelve, then increase to

half a deck, then a whole deck. In this way, you set small, realistic goals to accomplish your overall goal. Small victories will keep you going as you see your abilities improve.

2. **Person/Action/Object (a.k.a. PAO)** This step uses the technique of "chunking" information that you learned in the previous chapter. By taking 52 cards and dividing them into groups of 3, you reduce your list of 52 down to a manageable 17 (with one extra at the end). Person/Action/Object also takes advantage of the visualization technique previously discussed in Chapter 10. We'll start with the 12 face cards that you set aside before.

   a. Associate a person with each of the 12 face cards. It doesn't matter who the card reminds you of as long as it is easy to remember. Dellis says that the King of Clubs reminds him of Tiger Woods, because of golf clubs. King of Hearts reminds him of his dad, and King of diamonds reminds him of Donald Trump.

   b. Then decide on an action and an object for each person. For example, the King of Clubs is Tiger Woods, he plays golf, and his object is obviously a golf club.

   c. Once you have the idea of PAO (Person/Action/Object) for each card, you can group the cards into sets of 3. The first card will be the assigned Person, the second is its Action, and the third is an Object. This turns a group of three cards into just one image. For example, the three cards might be the King of Clubs, followed by the King of Hearts, followed by the King of Diamonds. You would picture Tiger Woods, doing heart surgery (the action), on a casino (the object).

3. **Use Your Memory Palace.** If things did not seem tricky before, they are about to. Here you use the memory palace technique you learned earlier in this chapter because you need a place to store each of the groups of cards as you memorize them. If your palace is your home and the first feature of your home is the lawn, you would picture Tiger Woods on your lawn, operating on a heart, on a casino.

4. **Expand to half a deck, then the whole deck.** Once you have been able to memorize the face cards, the next step is for you to figure out PAOs for each card in the rest of the deck. This can be tricky, so use your imagination. You can start by seeing if any of them are obvious to you. Assign significant cards to your friends, family and beloved pets first. Be sure to give each one a person, an action, and an object. For example, the 3 of Hearts could be your three-legged cat. The action could be eating, and the object could be cat kibble.

For the less obvious cards, the master memorizer Dellis suggests using something called the Dominic System, which is a code for numbers and suits that translates into letters, which then represents the initials of a person or character. We'll work through an example so you can grasp it.

The system:

The first 8 numbers are represented by the letters A through H, then the number 9 is represented by the letter N and the number 0 is represented by the letter O.

For the suits, Clubs = C; Diamonds = D; Spades = S; Hearts = H.

For example, Ace of Spades is an A and an S. Ace = A, Spades = S.
A.S. = Arnold Schwarzenegger/weightlifting/barbell.

5 of Clubs is E and C.
E.C. = Eric Clapton/playing guitar/guitar.

2 of Diamonds is B and D.
B.D. = Bo Derek (an actress, from the movie *Tommy Boy*)/braiding/hair.

So if you had the three cards together, in order, you would have Arnold Schwarzenegger, playing guitar on his hair.

You would place this rather odd image wherever it belongs in your memory palace so you know the order that you found it in the deck. This system is flexible and easy to personalize so that you can assign significance to cards as you see fit and as you will best be able to remember them.

5. **Practice!** After you put together all 17 sets of 3 (plus one extra), you may be able to memorize an entire deck

at your first try. To gain speed, all you need to do is practice, practice, practice! If you practice each day, you'll gradually cut your speed impressively as you gain the ability to recognize your assigned images and PAO for each card and gain confidence.

Seriously, Just Keep Practicing
With all of the techniques above and any amount of information that you wish to memorize, the key is "practice makes perfect." There's certainly no shame in sticking to the first 9 or 10 chapters of this book and using the tips to become the healthiest and sharpest version of yourself. Your memory abilities will be as strong as ever, and they will just keep improving as you eat healthier, exercise, get plenty of sleep and practice your meditation, creativity and emotional mindfulness.

However, for those who have lofty ambitions of conquering great feats of memory, it's time to embrace the techniques outlined in the last part of this guide. You'll find that with enough dedication and determination, you'll be impressing everyone with your memory prowess. Who knows, there could be a national or worldwide memory championship in your near future!

Conclusion

Thanks for making it through to the end of *Photographic Memory: 10 Steps to Remember Anything Superfast*. Let's hope it was informative and able to provide you with all of the tools you need to achieve your goals whatever they may be.

The next step is to put all that you have learned to good use! This is not the type of book that you can read and just put away if you want it to transform your life. Keep if available as a reference so you can use it as often as necessary. Keep trying the tips for nutrition, exercise, and sleep until you have found a good and healthy balance for your brain. Incorporate the meditation and mindfulness practices into your daily routines to maximize your awareness and further enhance your memory abilities. Don't forget to keep a busy and meaningful social calendar, especially if you are retired! Staying active is the key to retaining a youthful memory.

Next, keep trying different methods of creativity from Chapter 8. Find your own creative niche and prepare to be amazed as your creative endeavors enhance the power of your memory. Spend some time and effort in creating emotional awareness within you so that you can learn to appreciate your feelings but not allow them to interfere with your ability to recall experiences.

When you face an everyday memorization task, refer to Chapter 10 for help! With a little practice, you will find that you are able to remember your shopping lists, Christmas lists and daily appointments without writing them down. Finally, if you have goals of competing in memory challenges or you just want to see how far your own memory can take you, make Chapter 11 your bible. Find time in each day to practice the techniques described, and before long, your friends will be describing you as the one with the "photographic memory!" Don't worry, your secret is safe with us!

Finally, if you found this book useful in any way, a review is always appreciated!

Description

Have you been worrying that your memory may be slipping? Or are you envious of your classmate's apparent ability to memorize large amounts of information with ease? Perhaps you are heading towards the "golden years" and you just want to make sure you keep your memory sharp. Or you are about to start school after a long sabbatical and you want to be sure your study skills are up to par. If any of these describe you, or as the title suggests, you just want to develop a photographic memory for the fun of it, then *Photographic Memory: 10 Steps to Remember Anything Superfast* is the guide for you!

This informative book covers everything you need to know for boosting your brain health to optimize your powers of recall. From nutrition to sleep to meditation, you'll learn how to harness your brain's natural potential and impress yourself with your memory abilities. Did you know that tapping into your creative abilities can improve your ability to remember experiences? Or that a healthy awareness and acceptance of your emotions is critical to strengthening your memory?

In this revolutionary age of health care, we can all benefit from learning how to keep our minds sharp as we age. Not only will you learn how to improve your memory to its maximum, but you'll also learn the best ways to guard against the memory loss that can sometimes come with growing older.

You'll also learn tips and tricks of true memory champions. From techniques that will help you remember grocery lists with ease of learning how to memorize the first 100 digits of pi, this memorization book has it all.

Inside you'll find
- How to eat for better brain health and memory.
- The optimal level of sleep for your memory powers.
- The secrets to meditation and mindfulness to improve your recall ability.
- How to keep your mind active and memory sharp in retirement.

- How to harness your creativity to improve your memory.

- How to keep your emotions from mastering you and impeding your memory.

- How to memorize an entire randomly shuffled deck of cards in under two minutes!

And more

www.ingramcontent.com/pod-product-compliance
Lightning Source LLC
Chambersburg PA
CBHW071348080526
44587CB00017B/3010